T0355048

Stop
Giving
It
Away

Published 2015
Printed in the United States of America
ISBN: 978-1-63152-958-0
Library of Congress Control Number: 2015938904

Book design by Stacey Aaronson

For information, address:
She Writes Press
1563 Solano Ave #546
Berkeley, CA 94707

She Writes Press is a division of SparkPoint Studio, LLC.

Stop Giving It Away

HOW TO STOP SELF-SACRIFICING AND START CLAIMING YOUR SPACE, POWER, AND HAPPINESS

By

CHERILYNN M. VELAND, LCSW, MSW

SHE WRITES PRESS

Yesterday I was clever
So I wanted to change the world

Today I am wise
So I am changing myself

—RUMI

To my grandmothers, Hilder and Wanda,
two original Giveaway Girls

To Danetta and to all of the women who, like I do, feel as if they
may have been Giveaway Girls a time or two in their life

Table of Contents

AUTHOR'S NOTE

This book is written to help you develop a very high level of mental and emotional growth and health. Of course, it is not a substitute for professional mental health treatment. Many of the examples stem from my observations; however, in all cases, the person's identity has been changed to protect confidentiality. Because of my strong beliefs in ethical observance, if I were to have used any client/patient examples, I would have obtained client consent whenever possible. If you recognize yourself in any of the descriptions, it is merely a coincidence. After all, there are many of us out there who have been there before.

INTRODUCTION

I'm Cherilynn Veland, LCSW, MSW, a Chicago-area psychotherapist and clinical social worker. I have been counseling
people for twenty-plus years, and I love it.

Ever since I was a little girl, I have felt passionate about
fairness and helping others.

In high school, I thought I would go to law school and
advocate for the disenfranchised and struggling. But when I
had the opportunity to work in a law practice, I realized I
wanted to help people on a much deeper level.

Finally, in college, my "stop giving it away" career
trajectory ignited when I met Danetta. She was a seventy-five-
year-old African American woman who decided to leave her
abusive husband. She'd been married to him for sixty years and
had raised three children and many grandchildren before she
finally walked away. But first she cleaned the fridge, baked him
a casserole, and left him a note to say good-bye.

Working with the staff at a women's domestic violence
agency, I helped find Danetta housing and helped her carve the
path to a new life. But before Danetta left the shelter and
started that new life, we spent lots of time talking in the
kitchen of the shelter house. Late at night, we'd sit up together
in the darkened room, drinking coffee. I listened to her stories
about her life and about how she "gave it away," starting when
she was a little girl and up until this crucial time in her life. I
shared with her what I had learned about self-esteem, the
messages that press on us, and how we begin to form ideas of
our importance and place in the world.

I knew that being abused (and living with it) was an extreme example of giving it away. But something powerful happened in that kitchen with Danetta during those late-night talks: my awareness shifted.

I began to notice and think about a pattern that starts when we women are very young. I thought back to my childhood and all the messages that society had sent to me and how I had learned and accepted a lot of what had kept Danetta in that "Giveaway" place.

Danetta's situation helped me to understand that we women often spend too many years giving away the best of ourselves to the wrong relationships, bosses, circumstances, cruelties, even time. The reasons we do so are complex, but there are powerful societal forces that help bring about this pattern.

So, after Danetta, I watched, learned, listened, and paid even more attention to the shaping forces around me. I noticed these same forces affecting all of the women I met and knew. And I finally decided that I would write what I learned. After all, awareness is power. I want to pass along Danetta's gift to all of the women who were brave enough to accept it— hence this book.

Over time, I have learned that growth and change occur incrementally and that it's possible to claim our own space, power, and happiness—even at the age of seventy-five. I didn't know during those late-night talks with Danetta in that kitchen that twenty-four years later I would be dedicating my life to this work, as she would have wanted, but here I am.

Today, my work honors Danetta's courage to make her life her own. Sometimes I still think about her in the tiny new apartment that we moved her into. It was state-subsidized. When we moved her in, the kitchen came with these cute blue-checkered curtains hanging above her small window. On the day I said good-bye to her and wished her well, it was sunny and bright. I could hear birds singing, and I saw a bird fluttering right outside her kitchen window.

Thanks, Danetta.

CHAPTER 1

⁘

WHAT IS A GIVEAWAY GIRL?
WHAT IS GIVING IT AWAY?

"Most of the shadows of this life are caused
by standing in one's own sunshine."
—RALPH WALDO EMERSON

I know it when I see it. And I see it too often as a therapist and friend—a whole world out there full of Giveaway Girls . . .

Like Allison, a seventeen-year-old girl who won a full scholarship to NYU by studying hard and earning straight A's but abandoned her dream of going to college when she got pregnant.

Or Carla, who changed from an "I HAVE to go out with my homies on Friday night—BFF's are so important to me" girl into an "I'm busy with my boyfriend" chick who can't find time for her besties anymore. Her new boyfriend, John, takes up all her time and energy. She has disappeared from her girlfriends.

Or Drew, a secretary who, when her boss called her at eight o'clock one night and asked for a report she needed, took two buses in the middle of a snowstorm to get it to her—even though she didn't get paid overtime. In fact, her boss treats her like crap and she keeps trying and trying to get it right.

These examples may sound extreme, but the truth is, most of us have done some variation of what Allison, Carla, and Drew did. Millions of smart, together women unwittingly participate in their own self-destruction every day by engaging in this sort of behavior.

As a Chicago-based psychotherapist and social worker, I have dealt with a wide variety of mental health issues and life challenges. I've worked with battered women and sexual assault victims, have worked in psychiatric hospitals and in outpatient settings. I have also provided mental health counseling and substance abuse treatment to people within corporate settings and have offered workshops, training seminars, and crisis management services to a variety of for-profit and nonprofit institutions. For the past ten years, I have provided psychotherapy and counseling to individuals and couples in my private practice.

Through my work, I've learned that many of the anxieties and complexities within people's lives relate to their making decisions based on a codependent way of thinking I call detrimental caretaking (DC for short). This behavior leads people to feel anxious, depressed, and unhappy—both about themselves and about their relationships—and to experience job difficulties and an endless list of dissatisfactions. And this dynamic doesn't limit itself to the clinical setting.

For years I've been watching and paying attention to my life and the lives of those around me, and I have to say, I don't like what I see—DC in myriad forms. I see a world of women "giving it away" and a world in which women are coerced and cajoled into living in a destructive, harmful way. I see a world in which, little by little, women surrender their power and fundamental emotional rights as human beings. If you sometimes feel as if you are drowning in the needs of others, there's a good reason for it: you probably are.

Too many of us are Giveaway Girls. It's time we did something about it. Let's get started.

WHAT IS A GIVEAWAY GIRL?

A Giveaway Girl is a woman who betrays who she really is or what she really wants in life for the sake of someone or something else. She's someone who doesn't take good care of herself in relationships or her career—or in other parts of her life. A Giveaway Girl doesn't set good boundaries. She might even be the first to stick her neck out for someone else. She is that kind of person.

Giveaway Girls are usually great, caring, compassionate women—kind, nice, loving people—who unknowingly sacrifice important parts of themselves, usually for the benefit of others and to their own detriment. Sometimes a Giveaway Girl's "give-away" behavior is glaringly obvious. Sometimes it is less so. Regardless, by giving it away, Giveaway Girls cause a lot of damage to themselves and to those connected to them.

Knowing why we give it away is pivotal to disengaging with this behavior. We can't shake the power social constructs have over us until we know they're influencing us.

To understand the Giveaway Girl world, picture a wide, open field that you are required to walk through. You can't run through it freely, stopping to pick the wildflowers—you are stuck on a path, bound in by thorny bushes and thick vegetation on either side. The catch is, you don't even see the branches hemming you in; you can only feel them—and therefore, you will quite naturally stay right where you are supposed to. You can't see that this path is only one among other options that this open field has for you, because you don't realize that invisible forces are restricting you.

In life, women often follow a path like this one. It leads only to trouble, but so many other women are walking on it, we don't always realize that there's a big problem with the direction in which it leads us. That is part of the power of the social constructs with which so many of us cooperate.

It's not easy to stop participating in this system. After all, there are a lot of thorny bushes out there. To clear your own path, you need tools and a plan. This book will provide the tools; once you have them, it will be up to you to develop a plan that meets your needs and wants. You can do this. Believe me.

CAN A MAN BE A GIVEAWAY GUY?

Absolutely. In fact, as you look at the Detrimental Caretaking Lifeline ahead, it is important to note that it isn't always women who are detrimental caretakers. Some men out there are caring, compassionate, loyal, and awesome Giveaway Guys, who unknowingly behave codependently. They struggle too.

For example, some Giveaway Guys form relationships with women who don't consider their needs, or they connect with women who are dominating or unhealthy. These men may overfunction (usually through working too much). They don't set healthy boundaries or take good care of themselves.

Moreover, our ever-evolving society sends males conflicting messages about what it takes to be a good man in our society. It is difficult to be a woman in a man's world, but it isn't much easier to be a man in a man's world either.

I am fascinated with how our environment and societal expectations influence our decisions and behaviors. I believe that both men and women struggle with these codependent dynamics and that both genders, of course, deserve to get support and insight. However, we are socialized differently. Maybe the next book will be for the guys ...

ARE YOU A GIVEAWAY GIRL?

Yes, you probably are, but it's not your fault. If you're a woman, you have been conditioned since birth to sacrifice your own needs for the benefit of others. This tendency is probably so much a part of who you believe yourself to be that you don't recognize when you are doing it and don't understand how bad it is for you. Because of this conditioning, it is virtually impossible not to be "giving it away" in some area of your life—often without even realizing it's happening.

Women—quite naturally, and most times without even noticing it—frequently give up their wants, desires, energy, power, ideas, time, and dreams, mistaking doing so for being caring and compassionate. This process of giving it away is often subtle but very damaging nonetheless. Such behavior is always to your detriment.

IS EVERY WOMAN A GIVEAWAY GIRL?

Most women are. However, there are some exceptions. Women out there who aren't Giveaway Girls tend to fall into one of two categories: either they're healthy, balanced women who are conscious and aware of the tendency to give it away and have done a ton of work on themselves to combat it, or they're incredibly selfish and narcissistic.

The more we trend toward extreme detrimental caretaking (DC), the more discomfort we feel in daily life. What we give of ourselves feels increasingly out of balance. Putting first the needs, wants and whims of others becomes detrimental to our own well-being.

Detrimental caretaking: Where are you on this lifeline?
Which way are you trending?

Narcissistic women are the extreme opposite of Giveaway Girls. They're completely self-focused. They lack empathy for the needs of others. Thinking about others' needs and putting those first is very difficult for a narcissist. It's worth noting that narcissism is rarer in women than in men because women are usually socialized to think about others and steer clear of such selfish behavior.[1] Most Giveaway Girls fear becoming or being perceived as selfish and uncaring. Unlike the narcissist, the Giveaway Girl is more of a pleaser and thinks more about others than about herself.

The good news is that no matter how hard a Giveaway Girl tries, she will never become like the narcissist. Balance can be taught to a Giveaway Girl. Most narcissists, however, are disinterested in reversing their self-interested behavior.

Now, let's look at the second category of women. This category is underrepresented (right now, anyway). Women in this category live and work in a healthy, balanced world. I call them Got It Girls. They are conscious and aware of the Giveaway Girl dynamic.

Got It Girls are absolutely aware of the social constructs and pressures that try to shape their behavior in detrimental ways. However, they have done significant psychological work on their issues, and they strive every day to create balance for themselves. A Got It Girl makes conscious choices to be connected to her soul and her life, knows what she wants, and knows how to get it while still maintaining the relationships she cares about. She is able to healthfully detach when others strain against her boundaries and needs. She does self-sacrifice, but she does so with awareness and for the right reasons.

Most of us are still in the beginning phases of understanding how all our tendencies affect our day-to-day lives. So if you're a Giveaway Girl, don't waste time feeling bad or sorry about it—it's not your fault. A big part of what you are engaging in has been produced by the power of the social constructs that have been at work in the world for years and years (and years). It has been your legacy.

The idea here isn't to judge yourself; it's to cultivate a healthy, balanced life of your own. So before you go mentally identifying the women you know and putting them into the "healthy and balanced" Got It Girl category, keep in mind that you're probably being too quick to cast some girls into the "she's got it together" role. It is easy to see another woman and think she has her sh*t together, when in fact you are seeing only what she is presenting to the world. Chances are, she's giving it away somewhere.

People's lives always look different from the outside than they do on the inside—and, sadly, more women are giving it away than you might think.

CHECKLIST:
HOW TO SPOT THE GIVEAWAY GIRL IN YOU

If you think you might be a Giveaway Girl but are not sure, below are fifty questions to ask yourself. Circle the number next to any of the following that applies to you:

1. Are you a people pleaser?
2. Are you not a people pleaser in general, but you tend to be like that in intimate relationships (i.e., you don't want to rock the boat, make people uncomfortable, etc.)?
3. Do you tend to put others' needs before your own?
4. In general, do you treat people well and expect you will receive the same kindness and consideration from others in return?
5. Do you give other people the benefit of the doubt?
6. Does giving people the benefit of the doubt ever backfire on you?
7. Do you doubt yourself easily?
8. Can others easily make you question your own judgment?
9. Do you ever feel as if you have been "overemotional" or "selfish" when you finally get around to setting some limits?
10. Do you feel guilty when you try to set limits or boundaries that other people don't like?
11. Do you ever feel guilty when you indulge yourself in some way, especially if people are put out by it?
12. Do you feel guilty or bad when someone is mad or doesn't like what you have to say?

13. Do you keep your real opinions to yourself most of the time?

14. Do you avoid setting limits with certain people and tend to avoid conflict?

15. Do you have difficulty saying no, especially if you might come off as being mean or if there is any conflict that will arise from it?

16. Do you think that prioritizing your needs and wants, if doing so hurts the feelings of others, is selfish and unacceptable?

17. Do you frequently feel overwhelmed?

18. Do you have the "hurry sickness," or feel as if you have so much to do?

19. Do you have difficulty delegating to coworkers or family members?

20. Are you a procrastinator?

21. Do you ever feel used or taken advantage of in work, family, or relationships?

22. Do you ever feel as if the effort you put into relationships is unappreciated or unreciprocated?

23. Do you have the tendency to do too much or tire yourself out?

24. Do you find yourself doing more than just your share at work or at home?

25. Do you feel resentful about other people's lives?

26. Are you ever scapegoated in family, job, or work situations? (To be scapegoated means to be blamed unfairly.)

27. Do you suffer from depression or anxiety?

28. Do you ever feel victimized?

29. Do you feel as if you give more in your intimate relationships than you receive?

30. Do you frequently find yourself responsible for responsibilities, tasks, and other people?

31. Do you tend to feel overly responsible for other people's feelings?

32. Did you grow up in a family with addiction issues?

33. Are you susceptible to being manipulated by others?

34. Do you tend to obsess about slights that other people commit or that you perceive to have been committed against you?

35. Are you self-conscious about being liked, or do you feel a need to "fit in"?

36. Do you tend to be overly passive about asking for your needs to be met in relationships?

37. If someone disagrees with you, is it easy for you to think you might be wrong?

38. Do you feel anxiety when others are mad at you?

39. Do you sometimes not know what you are feeling?

40. Can you swing from being overly passive to overly aggressive?

41. Do you tend not to be direct, clear, and up front about your needs, wants, and desires?

42. Do you sometimes not know when your boundaries are being violated or not know when you are in need of something?

43. Do you have a tendency to feel very hurt or resentful if your unspoken needs, wants, or desires are not fulfilled?

44. Do you feel good about self-sacrificing and giving to those you care about but feel very hurt and frustrated when the same respect isn't given to you?

45. Do you have a tendency to self-sabotage? (In other words, do you end up blocking yourself somehow from reaching your goals?)

46. Do you ever try to overmanage aspects of your relationships?

47. Do you have a tendency to manage, fix, force solutions to, or overcontrol many aspects of your life?

48. Do people tend to lean on you or ask for your help a lot?

49. Do you often feel sorry for other people?

50. Do you have a great capacity for empathy with others but sometimes have difficulty empathizing well with yourself?

If you answered yes to at least five of these questions, you could be a Giveaway Girl—or maybe you know someone who qualifies. If so, you've come to the right book!

WHAT IS THE "IT" IN "GIVING IT AWAY"?

"It" is different for everyone. As I mentioned before, "it" could mean your time, your energy, your power, your dreams, or your desires. "It" could mean the freedom to do things you enjoy, honoring and exploring your true talents, or feeling comfortable being uniquely you. Sometimes "it" means your voice or your self-respect. Sometimes "it" refers to sex (that's what you thought of first, right?), but really, sex falls into giving-it-away territory only when you lose your self-esteem or self-respect in the process.

REAL-LIFE GIVEAWAY GIRLS

Giving it away is a little bit different for every woman. After all, we humans are so complex. As a therapist, and in my personal life, I've seen countless women "give it away."

Allison, whom I mentioned at the beginning of this chapter, was seventeen years old when she dropped out of high school. She had earned a full scholarship to NYU, but when she got pregnant, she gave up on school and got a job. After living as an uneducated, working, single mother for a few years, she tried again to get a college degree. Another guy came around (who treated her poorly), and she dropped everything to be with him for a while. It turned out he was an alcoholic.

How about Brook? She was twenty years old when her boyfriend talked her into getting new breasts because hers were "too tiny." Before dating him, she didn't think there was anything wrong with her breast size—and she later regretted having gotten the surgery.

Then there's Yvonne, a working mom who felt overwhelmed by everything she had to do to manage both her career and her children's lives. Her husband played golf all the time and did nothing to help around the house—and she didn't ask him to, even though she desperately needed the help.

Nastia, a Russian woman who immigrated to the United States in 1990, proudly showed me a picture of her twenty-year-old son the first time we met. She used to commute three hours a day just to drive him to nearby towns for his dance lessons, often sleeping in the backseat of her Chevy in freezing temperatures while waiting for him to finish. She and her husband both worked two jobs each just to support his dancing. "His dancing is my life," she told me. Six weeks later, I asked how her son's dancing was going. "He quit," she said. "He found a girlfriend and quit. I don't want to talk about it."

Mothers who focus so much on and give up so much for their children are Giveaway Girls, and there are a lot of them out there, too.

I've seen this compulsion to give it away in many great women—women with smarts and all the potential to have great lives. Part of this occurs because it's how they were taught to be. That's what makes it so hard to shake loose from this dynamic.

I have a copious amount of Giveaway Girl examples, and I will share many of them in this book. I challenge you to open your eyes a little and see how this dynamic might be playing out for you; you may even recognize parts of yourself in some of the women I describe. We will work through this together, and I am certain you will come out on the other side better armed and better able to manage your tendency to give it away. You can do it. You are much stronger and much more capable than you might think.

WHY IS GIVING IT AWAY BAD FOR YOU?

As I wrote this book, most of the people I told about it gave me overwhelmingly positive responses. However, some women—especially women who felt that, from a religious and/or spiritual perspective, sacrifice is part of living life well—challenged my Giveaway Girl theory.

"Aren't you promoting selfishness?" they asked me. This is a valid question—but the short answer is no, certainly not. Selfish people are just that. Giveaway Girls, in contrast, care wholeheartedly about others—so much so that they live too much for other people and neglect themselves needlessly. This imbalance inevitably leads to their hurting themselves and the people they care about.

Giving to others is not a problem in and of itself. The joy we receive from healthy giving can, in fact, provide deep and lasting happiness and peace. As a clinical social worker, I have dedicated my own life and work to helping others. In the process, however, I have discovered that caring and doing for others is not enough on its own; we also have to care and do for ourselves. When we don't, we limit our happiness and health and we compromise our ability to give to others.

Women who give it away may suffer from depression, anxiety, or unfulfilling relationships. They lose ground at work and are deeply affected in all kinds of negative ways. They suffer in their self-esteem and their self-value. In addition, when we don't satisfy our own selves in basic ways, that self-neglect inevitably leads to resentment and anger. Eventually, it hurts the people around us and the institutions we work in. We will talk more about the negative consequences of giving it away as the book progresses. Think about it a little like this:

Remember the airline instructions that direct us to put on our own air mask before trying to help our seatmate? It's the same idea here. You cannot tap into your deepest power until you have done for yourself first. My goal is not to teach women selfishness but to help them find a way to balance work and life, to get their needs met, and to enjoy freedom and healthier relationships.

I see women around me all the time who are tired, overwhelmed, depressed, and anxious—women who get more satisfaction from the bottom of their wineglass than they do from their daily lives. Much of this dissatisfaction and frustration comes from giving it away, which is closely tied to codependency. To truly understand what giving it away means, you first have to understand codependent behavior— what it means, and how it applies to you and your life.

The term "codependency" used to describe people who were related to drug or alcohol addiction systems, either through being in a partnership with an addict or through having been raised in a family within the alcoholic system.

Since its genesis, codependency has evolved from this early characterization to now include a grouping of unhealthy behaviors that result from dysfunctional family systems. Interestingly, many of these dysfunctional and maladaptive behaviors are encouraged and perpetuated in our society as a prescribed role for women.

CODEPENDENCY LANDSCAPE

Putting others' needs first and sacrificing for the good of others has always been expected of girls—much more so than it is of boys. Women's roles have traditionally been to support and sustain the lives of others. It's really only been in the past fifty years that women have begun to step away from having "supportive wife and mother" be their sole occupation.

Women have also traditionally had to be financially dependent on men, which in itself quite naturally breeds a sense of dependence and discourages self-reliance, and in turn encourages tolerating the intolerable as a survival mechanism. In addition, our naiveté about this fact holds up the social construct, keeping us on a confining path and pushing us to engage in harmful, codependent behaviors.

CODEPENDENT BEHAVIORS

There are numerous symptoms of codependency. Here are some of the most prevalent codependent behaviors:

- Poor self-care
- Picking unequal partners
- Being too dependent
- Not setting good boundaries
- People-pleasing
- Low self-esteem
- Being too passive or too aggressive
- Unearned guilt
- Denial

We will explore how our culture participates in this dynamic in Chapter 6, but for now let's explore these dysfunctional behaviors and see how they relate to women.

POOR SELF-CARE

People who are codependent tend to put others' needs first. When I refer to self-care, I'm not talking about taking time to do your nails. I mean having a healthy diet; exercising; nurturing yourself emotionally through positive, empowering thoughts; making healthy connections; getting support; and being kind and compassionate with yourself. If you're thinking, *Like I have time to read a book about how to treat myself better!* you're probably someone who could use a little more self-care.

Women have been taught that caring for others is more important than caring for themselves.

PICKING UNEQUAL PARTNERS

How many times have you met a woman who looks so much like she has it together—and then you meet her boyfriend/partner and he's a total jerk? How many great moms do you know whose partners don't participate equally as parents?

Awesome women have been picking not-so-awesome partners for a long time. Sometimes it is a reflection of low self-esteem, poor boundaries, or a lack of self-respect. Sometimes these women simply aren't demanding to be treated equally and setting healthy boundaries in the relationship. Whatever the reasons, when a woman passively tolerates an unequal partnership, it's a codependency red flag.

BEING TOO DEPENDENT

Unhealthy dependency on others definitely falls into the codependency category. What I specifically mean by "being too dependent" is surrounding yourself with people who aren't so good for you, or putting too much of your personal power into other people's hands.

Anytime you rely too much on other people's opinions of you or buy into the idea that you are more powerless than you are, you're being too dependent. Women can fall out of touch with their power too easily—especially because our society encourages them to do so. Research consistently shows women being viewed as less capable than men. We already know they make less money job for job. These messages send clear signals of being less than. It makes perfect sense for some of this to leak into our own subconscious.

Women are more susceptible to being overly dependent on others. This landscape (and I haven't even brought up the violence issue yet) would naturally result in the inclination to lean more on the people (or power) around them than to use their own strength.

We therapists refer to this natural, adaptive behavior as learned helplessness, in case you are curious.

NOT SETTING GOOD BOUNDARIES

Boundaries are limits we place on things, ourselves, and with others to help define who we are and what we want in life.

Boundaries are useful little accessories and we talk about them extensively in Chapter 8. Without them, one is a bit naked and vulnerable in the world. Unfortunately, most Giveaway Girls are bad at setting boundaries. I repeat: most Giveaway Girls are B-A-D at setting boundaries.

The reason for this is simple: good boundaries require setting limits, and setting limits can sometimes stir up conflict and hard feelings in others. Boundary setting and maintaining healthy boundaries can even seem painful at times. Most Giveaway Girls are conflict avoiders—or they are the opposite extreme, and they become in-your-face fighters when confronted. Neither one of these extremes is helpful. Setting and maintaining healthy boundaries are skills you need to live life well.

The trouble is, women are taught early on to cooperate and please at the expense of themselves, and this allows poor boundaries to pervade.

PEOPLE-PLEASING

Inherent in the term "people-pleasing" is the reason why it is detrimental to one's mental health. To want to please others is to try to meet their needs first. This involves being pleasant, going along with their line of thinking, and doing things not to rock the boat, usually so the pleaser will be positively regarded or awarded some sort of approval. It works—if you are doing, being, and saying what another person wants, they'll most likely be pleased. But at what cost to you?

Women are more likely to be people pleasers than men because they are taught from birth to be pleasant, pleasing, and less aggressive than their male counterparts. They must be more feminine. Young girls are given beautiful, passive women like Sleeping Beauty, Cinderella, and Ella Enchanted as role models. Boys, meanwhile, are given daring, adventurous characters like Jack (of "Jack and the Beanstalk") to look up to. Some of this is changing. At the time of this book's publication, there have been more powerful female hero figures represented in children's movies like *Frozen* and *Brave*.

Despite some progress on the Disney front, our society still has rigid and negative responses for women who don't engage in the behavior set forth for them (responses as simple but as devastating as using the dreaded "b-word"—"bitch"—to describe them, for example). People-pleasing is a surefire way to give yourself anxiety, self-esteem difficulties, and depression. How could it not?

To people-please is to subvert who you are.

LOW SELF-ESTEEM

In many ways, women's prescribed roles include a lot of automatic behaviors that indicate low levels of self-esteem. For example, just listen to the "I'm sorrys" you hear from women when they slip by you at Starbucks or on the street.

We women are the first to apologize for everything. Another example of these low-self-esteem behaviors might be our propensity to demur or devalue ourselves when we are complimented ("Oh, this old thing?"). In response to a job compliment, a lot of women might say something like, "Well, it wasn't a big deal." There are many complicated reasons why this happens socially, and I am not saying it is all bad. What I am saying is that there is a lot of behaving as if we have low self-esteem, and we're not consciously aware of it.

What about how women feel about themselves? Sure, that gorgeous woman in high heels walking down Madison Avenue looks like she's on top of the world. But how does she feel about herself when she's trying on bathing suits and looking at herself in a dressing-room mirror? How about when her boss, friend, or husband questions her decision making?

As a therapist, I've treated countless women who seemed at first to have positive self-esteem but then, on closer inspection, revealed that they often felt like failures or at least felt less than they projected to the outside world. In addition, it is extremely difficult to have completely positive self-esteem in a society that is set up to devalue you just for being female.

Lower self-worth established itself from early on in your life, even if you don't realize it.

BEING TOO PASSIVE OR TOO AGGRESSIVE

Being too passive or too aggressive in certain situations is a codependent characteristic—and it's a problem that many women have.

Many wonderful women are way too passive when it comes to tolerating not-okay behaviors from others. You probably know a few women around you who appear confident but allow their husbands to talk to them disrespectfully. They roll their eyes or hop to it to get their partners what they want, even if it isn't really okay.

Consider female leaders. In corporate America, they are consistently reviewed as either too passive (and therefore incompetent) or too aggressive (and therefore unlikable). This dilemma is called the "double bind"—an accurate name![2] Ultimately, falling too far on either end of the spectrum is going to be detrimental to your efforts. Being too passive in your relationships, or about owning your strength at work, or about asserting any of your needs, is not going to get you what you want, but taking a "guns blazing" approach isn't going to do it, either.

Giveaway Girls have to find a way to fall somewhere in the good middle: neither passive nor aggressive.

UNEARNED GUILT

Giveaway Girls often—and I do mean often!—feel guilty about things they shouldn't feel guilty about. These feelings are closely tied to shame, a devastating human emotion. For the purposes of this book, we are going to label this shame as unearned guilt.

Unearned guilt can rear its head when a Giveaway Girl tries to set a boundary by asking her partner to spend more time with her and less time with his or her friends—and then worries that she's being too needy or demanding. It can also surface when a mom has to deny her kid something he or she wants and feels bad about it, or when a professional leaves the office on time (rather than staying late) to get to a doctor's appointment, and a colleague makes a snide comment about her work ethic.

Mothers in particular often talk about guilt being the status quo in their lives. One friend of mine refers to this as "mom disease" and says every mom has it: we feel guilty when we don't take care of everyone else, and we feel guilty when we don't take care of ourselves—and then we feel guilty when we do.

Guilt is a vicious cycle and an undeniably codependent characteristic.

DENIAL

Have you learned to stuff down your feelings? Are you conditioned to push back your frustration, your disappointment, and your needs—so much so that it's essentially become a reflex for you, something you do without thinking? This is denial—yet another credit card in the Giveaway Girl's purse of codependency.

Giveaway Girls are often in denial about many things: how they are feeling, how they are living their lives, what's really going wrong in their intimate partnerships . . . even their own strengths. They put others' needs in front of their needs so frequently that they don't even notice they're doing it —and if someone tries to tell them they're giving it away, they deceive themselves into believing that it isn't true or doesn't apply to their situation.

Many women are in major denial about the impact that our cultural attitudes have on us. It's easy to overlook the ways in which our behaviors are consequences of the world we live in. It can also be hard to give up the self-defense that denial provides. In order for us to achieve a healthy balance in life, we have to drop the denial and meet our challenges head-on.

TRAUMA AND CODEPENDENCY IN WOMEN

Almost all women have been traumatized in some way in their lifetime. One in three women has experienced sexual assault, physical violence, or stalking by an intimate partner during her lifetime, according to the Centers for Disease Control.[3] And sexual assault and domestic violence are not the only ways in which people can be traumatized.

If you have been traumatized, you are much more likely to develop symptoms of codependency. This makes sense, doesn't it? Think about it. Many women have been attacked in some way just for being female—an experience that leads to an "I'd better conform and get along so I can stay safe" mentality. Certainly, this is not how all women respond. However, the power differential that is always present has to lay a foundation for some of this coping style. This kind of mentality plants the seeds for all the codependent behaviors we've discussed in this chapter.

The garden that our society cultivates is a vine-filled one that hems you in, holds you back, and can eventually become strangling. It leads to nothing good. Let's cultivate a new garden.

CODEPENDENCY AND PSYCHOSOCIAL DEVELOPMENT

I think it's important to mention here that I am not asserting that codependency or codependent behavior is caused solely by our society. Difficulty individuating and connecting with our authentic selves has multiple causes. Growing up or connecting with addictions, having attachment traumas, or not getting our normal developmental needs met as children, for example, goes a long way toward putting someone behind the emotional-development ideal.

What I am asserting is that we do not take into consideration our inherent socialization nearly enough when we offer up explanations and solutions for our self-defeating behavior. There is much literature out there that deals with childhood trauma and other such experiences and their effects on codependency—but there's very little on our social system as the root of some of this.

This book is meant to be a companion to the existing work on codependency. I encourage all of you, dear readers, to check out the resources mentioned in this book to add to your arsenal of knowledge and insight.

HOW TO MOVE FORWARD

A number of other dysfunctional behaviors fall into the codependency realm, but the behaviors addressed above are some of the most important ones for Giveaway Girls to acknowledge and work on.

You are not the crazy one! Women have been socialized to act codependently—then, when we act in these ways, we are told that we are neurotic and dysfunctional and have to change, but we are given no framework or direction for how to do so. Does that sound crazy-making to you? It does to me! No wonder so many women are more overwhelmed, anxious, and depressed than their male counterparts.[4,5]

Rest assured: these codependent behaviors are, for the most part, normal reactions to abnormal and unworkable social constructs. You're not the crazy one; our culture is. Our society is like an intricate web that traps women in these codependent roles—even though any mental health professional could tell you that engaging in these behaviors will surely lead you down an unhappy path. Together, we'll figure out how to break free of that web once and for all and create a life that feels better and is more manageable.

Let's start by talking about detrimental caretaking.

CHAPTER 2

⤜

WHAT IS DETRIMENTAL CARETAKING?

*"We must be careful in our decisions, careful in our words, and
we must be careful in our relationships . . .
we must live our life carefully."*

—NELSON MANDELA

M ost women are the caretakers of the world. Not sure about that? Let's take a look at the top twenty professions for women in the United States. For starters, they include nurses, teachers, secretaries, waitresses, and social workers—almost all of which are helping or service professions, in marked contrast with the top twenty male professions.[1] That isn't even taking into account the mothers and the caregivers (of the elderly and sick) of the world.

According to the research by the Family Caregiver Alliance, the monetary value of the informal care that women in the United States provide ranges from $148 billion to $188 billion annually.[2,3] However, no research can accurately compute all the help, nurturing, and kindnesses we women offer.

31

Women nurture. We care with our hearts. We feel and help. We do for others, often automatically. Society not only approves of this but pressures and pushes us in this direction. If those statistics don't convince you, I challenge you to go into a Toys-R-Us store and look at the aisles and aisles of pink caretaking equipment that little girls have to choose from. We women are taught to be nurturers and carers and that's powerful and positive in many ways.

I want to tell you about the other side of caring, the harmful side. It's called detrimental caretaking, and we women fall into the trap of it too often and too easily.

Having run a therapy and counseling practice; worked in psychiatric settings and for child welfare agencies and domestic violence and substance abuse treatment programs; and consulted for corporate and employee assistance programs, I've heard the dissatisfaction of women who work and live unnecessarily in a caretaker frame of mind. Their tendency to sacrifice for people and situations is what inspired this book. What I've found is that these women ultimately feel unfulfilled with their lives and are unhappy or unsatisfied with themselves.

WHAT IS SO DETRIMENTAL ABOUT DETRIMENTAL CARETAKING?

When it comes to people, some caretaking is a necessary and natural part of life (with children and the elderly, for example). It's what comes with being a caring, compassionate, responsible person. Caretaking comes from a great place of loving and giving. It's nothing to be ashamed of.

We become detrimental caretakers, however, when we:

- ✎ Take care as a result of unhealthy belief systems.
- ✎ Make decisions based on fear, pressure, and an inability to speak up for ourselves or because we can't set boundaries.
- ✎ Cover and do for people who can and should make decisions and take action for themselves.
- ✎ Take care of all these things first and at the expense— to the detriment—of ourselves.

We give of ourselves until it hurts. Harming yourself is never a good idea, and it's rarely useful for anyone else, either.

People who follow the detrimental caretaking path don't feel good about it, but it takes some effort and increased consciousness to realize the need for change. Detrimental caretakers take the inherent desire to nurture and be kind past the limits of what is okay. This is where the ideas of giving it away and Giveaway Girls really begin to take shape.

WHAT DOES DETRIMENTAL CARETAKING LOOK LIKE?

Can you relate to or do you know Giveaway Girls like: the mother who has a to-do list a mile long because she believes she has to, and there is no one else who can help; the girlfriend tolerating a bad boyfriend (he's more of a dependent than a productive partner); the employee who thinks she's being unreasonable or overemotional if she gets upset over the expectation that she carry more than her share of the workload; the woman who plays down her accomplishments at work because she doesn't want to hurt her colleagues' feelings; the employee who usually volunteers to watch the front desk when everyone else goes to lunch; the woman who makes decisions and action plans for a capable person who didn't ask her for help in the first place?

Detrimental caretaking occurs in different degrees and can happen in one or all areas of life—home, work, love, and so on. Detrimental caretaking means you give in (make sacrifices) for the people and circumstances around you. It can feel like something or someone other than you is running your life. It's important to identify detrimental caretaking tendencies in order to understand the power they may have over you.

The Detrimental Caretaking Lifeline

Studies confirm that as many as one in three women have been in relationships in which domestic violence has occurred. [4] Clearly, women in these relationships are Giveaway Girls to the extreme—and the reasons behind this role are complex. I worked extensively in battered-women's shelters, and everything I learned from those experiences suggests that surrounding pressure and power, combined with early life experiences (ranging from stressful to traumatic), ultimately disempower and lead many women into limited, self-sacrificing detrimental caretaking roles. These women cared greatly for the men in their lives, to their detriment.

Remember Danetta, the woman I introduced in the beginning of the book? At seventy-five, she decided to leave her abusive husband after being married for sixty years. She had spent a lot of time on the extreme end of the Giveaway Girl lifeline, stuck in a terrible situation.

EXTREME DETRIMENTAL CARETAKERS:

- Sense that they are in a bad situation with a bad partner but blame themselves or don't know when or what to do to change it.
- Appear unable to tolerate not being in a relationship.
- Are victims of domestic violence, often on repeated occasions and with multiple partners.
- Have been or are engaged in emotionally or psychologically abusive or damaging relationships.
- Find themselves repeatedly in severely dysfunctional relationships (with drug addicts, criminals, con artists, or other people living utterly reckless, unstable, or irresponsible lives).
- Have been frequently victimized.
- Often give up their power to others.
- Allow others to put them down (and put themselves down, too).

If you are in any of the situations above, stop right here. I encourage you to reach out for help. Confide in a trusted resource, a counselor, or a therapist. There are service organizations and twelve-step groups ready to help, too.

Most women fall somewhere in the moderate category. Their lives may be marked by chronic busyness and exhaustion. They're often running on empty, but they can't seem to get off that dial.

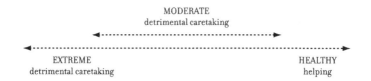

MODERATE
detrimental caretaking

EXTREME
detrimental caretaking

HEALTHY
helping

MODERATE DETRIMENTAL CARETAKERS:

- Complain that "there aren't enough hours in the day."

- Avoid conflict or saying no to others or to demands placed on them.

- Avoid saying yes to things that are good for them or things they want, if doing so means sacrificing others' needs for their own.

- Draw unclear or no boundaries between their own needs and the needs of others.

- Have no one to delegate to, or don't know how to delegate. Their motto is "I'll do it myself," but it stems more from helplessness or frustration than from empowerment.

- Have learned to skimp on or skip their basic needs— for well-being, nutrition, exercise, and rest.

- Base their identity and worth on giving to their spouse, or on their possessions, friends, jobs, or causes they lend their time to.

Detrimental caretaking is about giving it away to the point that we lose ourselves. Once we've lost so much, we're really not good to ourselves or to the people around us because we walk around feeling tired, sad, mad, and resentful. What are we giving away? Our energy, power, ideas, time, wishes, dreams, desires, comfort, and accolades—any one or more make up most of every person! Here's what Giveaway Girls do:

Meet Kara (again, not her real name). Her boyfriend, Andy, hasn't had a job in three years, and Kara feels sorry for him—he gets into fights with his boss and can't hold down a job. He talks about going to law school, but he doesn't make a move. He buys himself new things and has no trouble finding money for partying with his friends, but somehow Kara is the one who takes care of the bills and pays for everything they do together.

Now here's Janet. She works tirelessly, going far beyond her job description on a daily basis, not to mention picking up a ton of slack for her boss, Angie. Janet hasn't been promoted or gotten a substantial raise in years, and nobody else in the company knows that she handles so much of Angie's work. Janet feels sorry for Angie. Janet doesn't speak up for herself. Kara and Janet are rescuers.

In *Codependent No More*, Melody Beattie lists a number of ways in which we "rescue" those around us.[5] These include:

- Doing something you really don't want to do.
- Saying yes when you mean no.
- Doing something for someone even though that person is capable and should do it on their own.
- Meeting people's needs without being asked and before you've agreed to do so.
- Doing more than your fair share of work after your help is requested.
- Consistently giving more than you get back in a particular situation.
- "Fixing" people's feelings.

- Thinking for others.
- Speaking for others.
- Suffering consequences for others.
- Solving people's problems.
- Putting more interest and activity into a joint effort than your partner does.
- Not asking for what you want, need, and desire.

Giveaway Girls Don't Push Back

Kendall is an overscheduled wife and mother who has been putting up with her husband's selfish behavior for years—he golfs endlessly and hardly ever helps around the house—because the few times she's tried to confront him about it, he's flipped out. She doesn't want to upset the kids, and she believes it's easier if she handles everything herself. She's tired and cranky all the time, and she hates feeling that way, but she doesn't know what to do about it.

Arrianna is another great example of a detrimental caretaker. She's a hard worker, and not one to shy away from challenging opportunities at work, but she isn't good at receiving compliments, because she doesn't want to make any of her colleagues feel bad. So whenever anybody says something about how great her work is, she downplays it or tears it down. She feels like it's the right thing to do, but it leaves her feeling less than.

Think twenty-two is too young to be a Giveaway Girl? I've seen plenty of young women this age who have confided their frustration that their boyfriends won't spend enough time with them. But they never broach the subject, thinking that doing so will seem too needy. In fact the opposite might be true: she's making all the concessions to adapt her life to his schedule, and he's merely "fitting her in" after his poker game, his softball league, his nights out drinking with the guys. She ignores her frustration—and unwittingly falls into the trap of giving it away.

The women in these examples all make decisions based on an unhealthy belief system of detrimental caretaking. They believe downplaying or oppressing their needs for those of others is what's expected and generally okay, even if it doesn't really feel good in the long run.

Giving it away causes feelings of anxiety, sadness, resentment, and eventually anger. These women lose sleep, feel powerless, feel taken advantage of, and are generally dissatisfied with each turn of events.

Giveaway Girls don't know how to push back or even that they should.

GIVEAWAY GIRLS ENABLE, CONTROL, AND FIX

Therapists use the term "enabling" when you "help" someone to the point of preventing them from feeling any consequences for their actions. When you enable someone, you only "help" them to cause more damage through their bad behavior, choices, and decisions. This in turn inevitably leads to "fixing"—the ill-conceived actions we take when we try to prevent another's dysfunctional behaviors from harming others.

If my partner is a compulsive gambler and I work extra hours to replace the money he withdraws from our bank account for his binges, then I am enabling him and "fixing" the consequences of his bad behavior.

Other examples of fixing and controlling include:

- An overinvolved mom who makes doctor's appointments for her adult children, when they don't want her help.
- A woman who takes care of any problem at work, even if it isn't her responsibility. She might do this because she likes being in control or wants to be liked. Fixing will eventually backfire.
- Somebody who gives advice when she hasn't been asked.
- A well-meaning spouse or friend who fills a refrigerator with healthy food in an attempt to "get" the other person to eat healthier.
- A well-meaning friend who doesn't ask her alcoholic girlfriend to the cookout because she doesn't think her friend should be in the uncomfortable position of being around alcohol. Good intentions, but who gave her the green light to decide what was best for her friend's recovery? Her friend is an adult and can say yes or no to what she believes she can handle.
- The woman who attempts to smooth over or excuse her partner's grumpy mood or tries to "make it better."

RECOGNIZING DETRIMENTAL CARETAKING IN YOUR OWN LIFE

The examples I've given are just a few of the many ways in which women engage in detrimental caretaking. Unfortunately, the possibilities for how someone can give it away are endless. I can (and will!) give you snapshots of some of the situations I have observed in my life and practice, but ultimately you will need to learn to recognize for yourself the ways in which you fall prey to detrimental caretaking. If you're not sure you're capable of doing this yet, don't worry—as you read further and continue on this journey, it will become clear.

Detrimental caretaking stems from unhealthy beliefs. Can you relate to any of the following?

UNHEALTHY BELIEFS THAT PERPETUATE DETRIMENTAL CARETAKING

- It is my job to help, manage, or control other people, with their best interests in mind.
- I am doing this because I care and I believe I know what's best.
- It is selfish of me to turn my back on others, to not help whenever or however I can.
- It is mean to put myself first.
- If I can help someone else, I should.
- Just because I can do it myself is reason enough to do it all on my own.
- It is just easier and better if I do it.
- I am responsible for how others feel.
- I am stronger than they are.
- This is what is best.
- Putting myself first is selfish and mean.
- It is of paramount importance that others don't get their feelings hurt.

- If someone is mad at me, I must be doing something wrong.
- I feel bad for someone; therefore, I must help.
- He/she/they do not have a Higher Power or something greater that is caring for them and divining what they need in their life. Therefore, I must get involved.
- It is my job to help them feel better.
- I can figure out a way to get them to . . .
- I am not powerless over their addictions or their ....
- Avoiding conflict is best.
- I can be happy if I can just get .... to change.
- Peace is the absence of conflict.
- I can handle this; they can't.
- My religion and spiritual beliefs tell me that not putting others first is wrong.

As with most of our beliefs, you may not realize this is how you think or that these thoughts are governing your everyday life choices. All or some of these may even sound reasonable, but keep reading because you need to know how these ways of thinking can hurt.

HOW DETRIMENTAL CARETAKING HURTS EVERYBODY

All of the women you've read about so far are wonderful women who care for the people in their life the best way they know how. Their detrimental caretaking behavior, however, is not helpful—in fact, it's only causing harm. If you are a detrimental caretaker:

- You're perpetuating or ignoring the destructive or dysfunctional behavior of the other. When you allow this kind of behavior to go unaddressed, you end up not helping at all.

- You're preventing people from feeling the consequences of their behavior. Without consequences, people have no motivation to change their bad behavior.

- You're preventing the person, organization, group, or system from confronting and correcting deep-seated problems. Doing things ourselves—experiencing the good and the bad, the hard and the soft, even failing— makes up an important part of our lives. It's what allows us to learn and grow.

- It's condescending. When you do something for someone else, you let them know by your behavior that you don't think they can handle things on their own.

- It causes you to feel resentful, steamrolled, and taken advantage of. Eventually, these feelings will damage your relationship with the person or the organization you're trying to "take care of."

- It makes you feel angry and/or exhausted. Over time, detrimental caretaking will cause you to develop a bad case of CDR—codependent depressive rage—which we'll cover in Chapter 4. This is not pretty and is certainly not good for anybody you care about.

WHAT IS HEALTHY HELPING?

Healthy helping is the opposite of detrimental caretaking. Healthy helping is where you want to be. Here, decisions are good for you and for others. Learning to stop giving it away isn't about "me first"—it's about "me too."

Healthy helping is about sacrifice, extended effort, and proactive compassion—but cast within sensible limits.

Healthy helping doesn't require us to sacrifice our health, personal boundaries, or emotional well-being; in fact, healthy helping contributes positively to all of those areas. Notice the characteristics that the following examples have in common:

- Helping an elderly lady with one hand on a cane cross the street with a bag of groceries. Ideally, this feels good for you, has a positive consequence for her, and doesn't leave you exhausted (unless, of course, you try to carry her piggyback-style!).

- Voluntarily taking on additional tasks at work because one of the staff members had a heart attack and would miss his project deadline if you didn't help out.

- Listening to a coworker who is usually very positive complain about her stressful weekend. You rarely hear this coworker complain, and you can tell she needs a listening ear over coffee—plus, you know she will be there for you when you need the support, too.

- Buying your boyfriend a watch that he has been wanting because it is within your budget and you want to make him smile.

- ⁕ Donating or tithing money to your church, a favorite charity, or your daughter's school as a part of your monthly budget allowance because it feels good knowing you are making a difference.

- ⁕ Donating time to a charity, your church, or your daughter's school, instead of a monthly tithe, because you can't afford to give money but still want to help.

- ⁕ Joining the welcoming committee at your daughter's school to help attract more students because you feel good about it and are able to budget your time to do it.

- ⁕ Stopping and helping a lost stranger with directions.

- ⁕ Giving money to (or buying a sandwich for) a homeless man begging for donations—or, if you have nothing to give, acknowledging him with respect and continuing on your way.

- ⁕ Forgiving your husband for forgetting to get you an anniversary gift because you know he's been under additional pressure at work, and he's never forgotten before—he honors you in so many other ways that you can uncritically forgive this unintentional blunder.

- ⁕ Helping with the reading group at your son's school and making cupcakes when asked to volunteer to bring sweets to the May Day celebration at school.

- ⁕ Bringing a skinny, homeless puppy to a shelter and paying for his shots.

- ⁕ Allowing your spouse, partner, or friend to be in a bad mood and not worrying about it yourself. You are giving them space to be who they are.

- ⁕ Volunteering to teach Sunday school because the kids make you laugh.

THE GOOD SAMARITAN AND THE GIVEAWAY GIRL: A PARABLE

My parents raised me on biblical parables, most notably that of the Good Samaritan. If you're still confused about the distinction between healthy helping and detrimental caretaking, maybe this will help:

A Samaritan walks by a beaten man and sees that he needs help. Unlike the others, who have passed the man by without a second look, the Samaritan tends to his injuries, gives him shelter, and saves his life.

So, was he giving it away?

No! Somebody who needed help got it from a man who was willing and able to give it. Now, if the Good Samaritan had exhausted himself to the point of illness by helping others, especially those who could help themselves, it would be a different story entirely. But he was in a healthy, strong place, and he used his kindness, strength, and courage when someone on the brink needed it most.

Now imagine a Giveaway Girl in the Samaritan's place. She's likely too exhausted and irritated to help—or she doesn't have the cash to help the guy because she's just helped her boyfriend with his luxury chariot payment. Or perhaps she whizzes past the poor victim because she's late to go take care of somebody else's emergency.

She sees the man lying on the ground and grits her teeth. "Are you kidding me?" she says. "I've gotta take care of you, too? I can't do it all! I'm taking care of Mary's kids, supporting my boyfriend, doing the work of three people in the fields— and, to boot, I've gained forty pounds from bingeing on unleavened bread. I'm exhausted. When is somebody gonna help me?"

Sound like a mean response? If you didn't know her whole sad story, this Giveaway Girl would seem self-centered. After all, anyone who turns up her nose at an injured man in the road isn't acting kind, nurturing, or respectful. But the truth is, she's not selfish—she's just used up. She's given away too much to too many people in too many situations, leaving too little inside her to do any good. And much of the giving away she did was unnecessary. She just couldn't see it. Can you?

Cutting the Chaos and Creating Balance

Trying to discern the difference between healthy helping and detrimental caretaking all boils down to one essential question: Have I made a conscious decision? Or, as inspirational coach Heath Howe puts it, "Am I living by conscious choice?" I'll add, are you at peace about your choice?

If you fully see the decisions you make, understand the consequences, can tolerate the risks, and consciously choose to extend yourself for another, that's one thing. But if you're doing damage to yourself unknowingly—because that's all you know and you don't believe you have other choices—that's another matter entirely, and it shows that you've adopted a destructive pattern. Like a true Giveaway Girl, you feel like you just can't help yourself—but you can.

Ask yourself: Did I really, really want to do what I just did? How do I feel now that I've done it? Am I choking back nagging anxiety, discomfort, a touch of regret, or even a sense of foreboding? If you've just rescued, fixed, or enabled, your answer to that last question is almost certainly yes—because what comes after detrimental caretaking isn't that satisfied, comfortable, pleasant feeling you get when you've helped someone who needs it; it's an undeniable backlash, often signaled by a knot in your stomach and a dull ache in your heart.

Nurturing others is important, but there's a huge gulf between healthy helping and detrimental caretaking. Let me emphasize: there's a big difference between helping, nurturing, and loving others and engaging in detrimental caretaking.

Detrimental caretaking creates personal chaos. It leads to burnout, exhaustion, anxiety and unhappiness. It drains you emotionally and spiritually. Healthy helping cuts that chaos and creates an environment designed in balance. How do we change our patterns and live life better? We'll get into that later in the book. Giveaway Moms are up next.

CHAPTER 3

✐

GIVEAWAY MOMS

"All that I am and all that I hope to be,
I owe to my angel mother."
—ABRAHAM LINCOLN

When women become mothers, the self-sacrifice starts immediately: their bodies, their sleep, their time, their careers . . . I could go on and on. The thing is, in the beginning, the self-sacrifice comes easily. It can even feel good.

SELF-SACRIFICE COMES TOO EASILY

Being a mom is, to put it mildly, a tough job—and if you get into the habit of giving too much of yourself early on, it can be difficult to learn where to draw the line between being a good mother and giving it away.

It's incredibly important that all moms start thinking more about finding a healthy balance between their needs and the needs of their children. In this chapter, we'll discuss the many ways in which mothers fall prey to detrimental caretaking—

and why—and what they can do to disengage themselves from this damaging cycle.

SOCIETAL PRESSURES AND MOTHERHOOD

Before we look more into the issues of self-sacrifice and detrimental caretaking as they relate to motherhood, we first have to understand the context within which women today make their mothering decisions. A lot of what we decide to do and not do as mothers has to do with what we understand our role in society to be—and the complex messages we receive about motherhood on a daily basis have a negative effect upon our ability to make balanced decisions.

These messages are especially damaging because they're so insidious—because they affect us without our realizing it. We unconsciously internalize these messages and listen to them. It is impossible to develop a healthy balance in your life if you aren't aware of the pressures and external determinants that affect your decision making. Let's examine what some of these messages are, starting with the devaluing of the role of motherhood.

"Motherhood is so important—but not really."

On the surface, society embraces the idea that motherhood is a worthwhile and noble occupation—but lots of messages suggest just the opposite. Just look at where we as a country are willing to invest our money: we pay child care providers minimum wage, but we pay the people who pick up garbage at least three times that. Teachers (primarily women) make substantially less for a living than people in other public-sector jobs. Everywhere you turn, there are subtle (and sometimes not-so-subtle) indications that child rearing really isn't that important or that impressive a job.

Sure, you will hear the occasional political speech or church sermon in which mothers are lauded for their efforts— and, of course, you will hear a big round of applause on Mother's Day. But ask your average homemaker how she feels at a cocktail party when somebody asks what she does for a living, and she'll probably tell you that she feels judged or looked down upon in some way. We've all heard people laughingly making fun of stay-at-home moms: "What do they do all day, anyway?" The signs are everywhere, and their message is this: motherhood, on its own, is not enough. I strongly disagree with this notion, but these are the messages mothers receive over and over. This impacts how we feel about ourselves without our even knowing it.

I have met with many stay-at-home moms as clients who have reported sensing negative judgment directed at them from the outside. They sense that others don't really value what they are doing, even if they themselves truly do. Some research shows a higher incidence of depression, sadness, and anger among these stay-at-home moms.[1] The reasons for this reaction are complicated, but some of it may come from the lack of value our society places on this generous job.

"Being a bad mother is the absolute worst thing a human being can do."

When it comes to motherhood, there is no rulebook telling us what's good versus bad—but historically mothers have been held fully accountable (and therefore fully blameworthy) for the physical and emotional health of their children.

In the past, psychological professionals asserted that the strength of the bond between a mother and her child is solely responsible for that child's psychological health. Mental illnesses that now have a clear biological component used to be linked with the inability of a mother to bond appropriately with her child, and homosexuality used to be deemed an aberration created by a mother who "feminized" her sons by being overly attached to them.[2] Even autism has been blamed on a mother's attachment style.[3] Freud, the father of psychology, asserted that a mother biologically (and automatically) knows how to care for her young. Luckily, some of that has changed, and research is emerging to give more balance to this topic.

However, pressure is still there to constantly reach an idealized role of perfect mothering—and that lays the groundwork for women to give it away to the extreme.

> *Even kids blame moms for an enormous amount. Ask any mom of a teenager. This is partly normal psychological development, as well as a reflection of our societal expectations of mothers.*

In some ways, I am glad we feel pressure to be the best we can be as mothers. Raising small, innocent beings who start out completely physically and emotionally dependent on us is an enormous responsibility. A mother's nurturing and care have a tremendous impact on a child's well-being and sense of self. But the "ideal" mother is a myth—one that both puts too much emotional pressure on the mother and devalues the role of the father in a child's psychological growth.

When Giveaway Girl mothers feel as if they are completely responsible for their children's welfare, the obvious outcome is that they can take on more than they should, thereby exhausting themselves and preventing their partners from taking a more active role in parenting. This is understandable: when so much is leveraged onto one person, it's hard to let go. Plus, a lot of men out there are not willing to pick up the ball and meet their partners halfway—an issue we'll discuss more in depth later in this chapter. However, caving to society's pressure to assume responsibility for everything—accepting the "ideal" mother myth as reality—plays out to everyone's detriment.

Acknowledging that you can't do it all is an important step toward making more balanced decisions for yourself and your family.

"Self-sacrifice is the definition of good mothering."

When I told my ninety-two-year-old grandmother about my book, she was aghast at the concept that self-sacrifice could be construed as a bad thing. "That's what being a mother is," she exclaimed, "it's all about sacrifice!" She was visibly upset by the idea that her own approach toward mothering—the premise of which was self-sacrifice—might have been wrong in some way. Later, when I asked her for examples of times when she may have gone a little overboard in putting others' needs first, she couldn't think of any. Luckily, my aunt piped in.

"Mom, what about when you were pregnant with your second child? I thought you stopped eating and were working so hard on the farm that your teeth started to fall out," she said.

"Oh, yes," my grandmother said. "But they didn't fall out—they just got really loose in my gums."

The woman can rationalize anything. We women can rationalize our overboard caregiving just as easily.

Most Giveaway Girls have grown up in a world in which they have been taught to give to and sacrifice for others. When you add motherhood to the mix, you can end up with someone who self-sacrifices to the point where it becomes detrimental—and that's not good for anyone involved.

When the needs of your children are ever present, where and when can you make the decision to self-nurture? How do you give your kids what they need while maintaining your individual emotional integrity? Can you recognize the difference between your child's real needs versus wants? Do you allow yourself to be manipulated? How do you draw the line between caretaking and detrimental caretaking?

GIVING IT AWAY, MOM-STYLE

Finding the right balance in your life isn't something you can do overnight. You can start, however, by learning to identify the difference between being a good mother and giving it away. As you read about the common ways in which mothers act like Giveaway Girls on the following pages, think about whether you engage in any of these behaviors. If you recognize your own situation in any of the dynamics explored here, it may be time to take a different route on your path.

STAYING TOO BUSY

A few years ago, on a brisk but sunny fall day, I accompanied my son's preschool class to Chicago's Swedish American Museum for a field trip. During the visit, the museum guide brought us to a "Swedish farmhouse," where—as my son and his classmates ran around, pretending to milk cows—she told me and the other adults present about the difficult work life of a Swedish family during the 1800s. She described the apple masher they used to make applesauce; she pointed out the limited kitchenware (a wooden bowl, a few chunks of wood that resembled plates, and one big wooden spoon); she helped us to envision the difficult stove they used, which took hours to heat up.

As the guide waxed on about the ins and outs of life on a farm in the 1800s, I was initially horrified. It took about five hours just to cut, churn, and mash apples into applesauce. How in the hell did these poor women wash clothes, make bread, not burn everything, and take care of their kids at the same time, stuck in that tiny room, for the whole winter? I wondered. *Thank God*, I thought. *Thank God I am not living back then.*

As I looked at the faces of the mothers standing around me—smiling and shaking their heads in consternation at the plight of the nineteenth-century Swedish farm wife and mother while simultaneously keeping one eye on their children—I came to a terrible realization: most moms are just as busy nowadays as those frontierswomen were two hundred years ago. When was the last time we didn't all have a long list of things that needed to get done? We don't have to stand there in a crude dress, mashing apples for five hours, but we are still running like mad from one task to the next. Mothers today are still overwhelmed and overtasked—still short on time. How can it be that everything has changed but nothing has really changed?

Modern conveniences—dishwashers, cars, cell phones— were supposed to "free" us, but it seems they haven't done their job. Just look at the cover of any magazine targeted at moms: "How to Get Better Sleep!" "How to Get More Done in Less Time!" "How to Deal with a High-Stress Life!"

Clearly, many women are working way too hard and doing way too much. Somehow, we mothers have gotten it into our heads that this is how it is supposed to be—but that's simply not true. Being sleep-deprived and overtaxed is not our only option.

For some women (often single mothers), circumstances present significant challenges and heavy burdens that make it necessary to live and work in these ways just to survive. After all, the majority of the world's poor are women and mothers. [4] And one-third of women in the United States are living "on the brink of poverty."[5] In these cases, we should look at the failing systems around these women and their children and see how we as communities and support networks can do better.

For most other women, feeling the need to be so busy doing for others is just that—a feeling, a pull—not really the need we think it is.

TAKING CARE OF EVERYONE ELSE FIRST

Society tells us—in ways both subtle and overt—that a self-sacrificing mother is a good mother. But too much self-sacrifice leads to burnout. Just look at Kathy and Emily, two moms who spend so much time taking care of everyone else that they have no time for themselves.

~ *Kathy* ~

Kathy is forty-five, owns a successful real estate company, and has three kids and a husband. She is really the breadwinner, although her husband does have a full-time job.

Kathy always looks put together: high heels, sharp suits, flawless makeup, great hair. She drops her children off at school in the morning (even when she has meetings until seven the night before and her husband's slate isn't exactly full). Kathy is also an active participant in a number of school-related committees. At least twice a month, she hosts ten to twelve kids and their mothers for a playdate at her house, where she serves pizza and cocktails—and she never lets anyone help tidy up before they leave, even though her home is a wreck afterward. She enjoys the playdates but sometimes wonders why no one reciprocates.

Kathy usually goes to bed way too late, and when she finally does lie down, she feels exhausted and anxious, worrying that she must have forgotten something. Her husband golfs a ton and doesn't talk much, but it's too difficult for her to contemplate doing anything about it—it always ends up in a fight, and then she just feels guilty. She can't remember the last time she had a vacation.

From the outside, Kathy appears to have a great life. She owns a successful business, has a husband and children, and is active in the community, and still she manages to look great. Her business peers respect her, as do the moms in her school circle. But Kathy isn't happy—and that's because she's giving it away.

Does Kathy really want to spend so much time on the committees at her children's school? Is it really healthy or positive for her to work until 2:00 a.m. every night? And how about those playdates? Does she really need to spend the last half hour of her evening cleaning up crumbs and vacuuming the playroom? Finally, does she truly feel fulfilled in her relationship with her husband? Is she really okay with doing all the work all the time?

Kathy tries to delegate as much as possible; she tries to make time for herself. But somehow the occasional manicure or glass of wine with her friends doesn't seem to help much. She feels as if she's trying to fix broken bones with bandages. She knows she's doing too much—but the prospect of change terrifies her.

~ Emily ~

Kathy cuts Emily off at the entrance of the school as she goes to drop her kids off—and as she flings the heavy door open, it slams into Emily's stroller. Kathy's in too much of a rush to notice, but Emily thinks Kathy's brushed by her on purpose, and boy, is she pissed. Why doesn't Kathy ever make eye contact with her or introduce herself? Emily's tried to say hi to her on multiple occasions, and Kathy has never responded, except for a meek wave one time. (*Stuck-up bitch*, Emily thinks.)

It doesn't help that Kathy's impeccable appearance makes Emily feel so insecure. She's been up since 3:00 a.m. because her son wet his bed again, which means Emily had to get up and change the sheets in the middle of the night for the sixth time in as many days—but even so, she barely had time to take a shower this morning, and she was too tired to put on makeup before she left the house. Emily always feels uncomfortable without it, but she just didn't have the energy.

Emily's husband has a full-time job as a lawyer at a major firm, and things have been really stressful for him lately—she can see the strain in his face when he comes home from a long day—so she hates to wake him at night to help her with the kids. Anyway, he only makes things harder.

"What do you want me to do?"

"Feed the baby, John."

"But I can't see . . . it's too dark in here!"

Sometimes Emily wants to scream, *You graduated from law school, John—why do I have to tell you how to turn on the light?* But she knows she shouldn't blow up at him like that. She's his rock. Besides, she's better with the kids anyway. She loves being a mother. So it's best if she just gets up, takes care of any problem quickly, and gets right back to bed. That way, she can get another hour of sleep in before she starts breakfast for everyone.

Emily usually spends several hours a day playing with her kids. If her daughter wants to play dolls, she plays dolls. If her son wants to play with Legos, she does that. Sometimes when she's playing with her kids, she daydreams about her former job as a consultant—how good she felt about herself, the pride she felt when she gave her team a great idea or completed a difficult project. She's proud of her work at home, but she sometimes feels bored.

Emily enjoys being a mother and is grateful for her two healthy children, but her demeanor and physical appearance betray an exhaustion that runs deeper than just lack of sleep. Emily wants her old life back, or some part of it. As a consultant, she thinks in project outlines. Why can't she just outline things better? Why does she feel so bad sometimes?

Emily doesn't want to be the only one responsible for the physical and emotional care of her children—and sometimes she wishes she had more time to do her hair and makeup, or at least work out a little. But when she tries to discuss this with her husband, he gets upset: "What do you want me to do,

Emily?" She doesn't know. She decides to keep doing what she's doing. Maybe things will change as the kids get older. But when? How? *I just need to try harder,* she tells herself. *I'll figure this out someday.*

Until that vague, undefined day arrives, Emily will be stuck giving it away.

You probably don't fit exactly into the example of either Kathy or Emily. But we've all been guilty of taking care of everyone else first at some time or another. Other examples of detrimental caretaking might include the mother who has gained a ton of weight and is unable to lose it because she is too busy; the mother who buys nice things for her kids but never for herself; the mother who allows herself to be treated unequally or without respect by her husband; the mother who dedicates tons of hours volunteering at school because she feels bad about not having a "real" job; or even the mother who always cancels get-togethers with friends because her husband "can't handle" getting the kids' homework done. She feels like she has to be there to fix, manage, and control.

Essentially, giving it away as a mom is when others come first and you come way last.

DIM SYNDROME (DO IT ALL MYSELF)

Just because you can do it all doesn't mean you should. Let me repeat that: *just because you can do it all doesn't mean you should.* But most women, and especially mothers, don't ask for enough support.

Take Alice. She was so good at doing everything. Her husband began to expect that she would always do it, no matter what the situation. So when the car got snowed into the garage and wouldn't budge, her husband came to her to take care of it. "We need to push it," she told him—so he got into the car and patiently waited for Alice (who is half his weight) to do the work. Alice had been pushing the SUV for a while before she realized the hilarity of the situation and got her husband to switch places with her.

This is what Giveaway Girls do: they give and give and just keep plodding down the trail with everybody's stuff on their back. They do it all; they manage it all. They push the freakin' car! Luckily, Alice had the good sense to learn from that experience. She began examining, in therapy and on her own, how she had ended up being the one who did it all. She slowly started implementing some power shifts in the family, stepped back from doing it all (that was *hard!*), leaned more on her husband, and requested help from her family members and other people. She let her house get messy once in a while. And she started reading again, even if that meant sitting her kids in front of the TV for an hour so she could do it.

Not everyone learns as quickly as Alice did. Statistics show that women—even those with full-time jobs—still take on most of the families' child care duties in the United States. In addition, they do almost double the housework their male partners do on a daily basis.[6]

I interviewed a respected colleague, who is also a mother, about mothers' tendencies to do too much, and she said she thought mothers sometimes wear their self-sacrifice like a badge of honor. She described waiting in line with the other mothers at her children's school at pickup time: the moms often talked about how overwhelmed they were and all the things they were in the midst of doing that day—but they did it in a competitive way. There was lots of laughing and joking, but with an underlying tension regarding who had given more.

A lot has shifted since our mothers' time, but their legacy filters down into our mothering styles—some of it good, some of it not. A lot of middle-aged Giveaway Girls have mothers who were martyrs. The idea that martyrdom is a positive quality is something to set aside—and if you're not in the habit of thinking about this stuff, you're probably engaging in some martyr-like activities yourself. This brings me to the next dynamic that Giveaway Moms fall for.

HELPLESSNESS AS MANIPULATION

Because Giveaway Moms are used to having to do everything themselves, they eventually begin to think that others are less capable then they are—and then they fall for people's apparent helplessness as an invitation for them to take over and "just do it myself."

Take, for example, the Peanut Butter Sandwich Incident:

Carmen, a new mother, was getting very depressed, exhausted, and agitated from lack of sleep. Finally, she asked her husband, Paul, to do the eleven o'clock feeding one night so she could catch up on some rest.

Like clockwork, little Samantha started to yowl right at 11:00 p.m. Carmen waited a few seconds before nudging her husband. "Honey, the baby is up. She needs you."

"I got it," he grumbled. He got up and headed into the kitchen. After hearing lots of puttering around and cabinets opening and closing—the baby still crying—Carmen was wide awake. She got up and walked to the kitchen, and there was her husband . . . eating a peanut butter sandwich. The bottle was sitting on the counter, ready to go.

"Why haven't you fed the baby?" Carmen yelled.

"I'm going to," her husband muttered, still chewing. "Relax! I was hungry; I made myself a peanut butter sandwich first. Jeez." Before Carmen could react, he plodded off with the baby bottle in his hand.

Carmen was so upset by this. It made her just want to jump in there and do it herself! In addition, Carmen's frustration began to kill her willingness to ask her husband to help her in the future. But you see, Giveaway Moms, that is exactly the results you don't want to have happen.

When people (or partners) act helpless or clueless about what it is you want or need; they are trying to get you to pick up the problem. And Giveaway Moms fall for this all of the time. Don't fall for it.

Paul probably wasn't manipulating Carmen or shirking his responsibilities intentionally. Manipulating someone doesn't require intent; people do it unconsciously all the time. The results are the same as if they'd done it on purpose. And partners aren't the only ones who manipulate Giveaway Moms; kids do it, too, acting helpless and needy in order to get their moms to do what they want. And it usually works—after all, Giveaway Moms are caring, compassionate women who don't want to see anyone in pain, especially their own children.

My own children have been known to try it a time or two —in fact, as I am working on this very chapter, they keep coming in and demanding that I "help" them. My youngest, age five, wants help putting together the last Lego man in the Lego station ship. The oldest, age ten, just yelled from the kitchen that he is "putting together a story like 'The Old Lady and the Shoe,' except I am using a fly and some plastic bags," and that he needs me to come assist him.

I'm tempted to go running to both boys' aid—but I have only an hour set aside to do my writing, and I am suspicious that both of these pleas for help are merely the catcalls of bored children. So I'm not falling for it—not even when my five-year-old throws a fit and tells me I'm "mean." And it's not just about putting my own needs first once in a while— research shows that kids' ability to do things and feel competent is a big factor in positive self-esteem and independence. If you spend all your time giving, rescuing, and caretaking, your kids won't get the opportunity to build those skills.

So what have I learned from all this? It's nice writing from home sometimes—but next time I want to get some work done, I think I'll head to my office.

ENCOURAGING DEPENDENCY

Since giving it away falls into the realm of codependency, what does that look like in motherhood?

In the world of moms who act codependently, everything else goes away—their sole focus is on their kids. Here's Sheila. Her life revolves around her daughter. Sheila can't tear herself away from overfocusing on this relationship and feels needed all the time. Sheila's daughter feels this tremendous need and pressure, even if she isn't consciously aware of it. Sheila's smothering has a big impact on her daughter's independence, confidence levels, and sense of self. In addition, Sheila is cutting out important opportunities for connection and growth in her own life. But, she can't see it. She is giving it away, and she continues her codependent behavior into her daughter's adulthood.

Being a mother is an extraordinarily important job. If we derive all of our value from motherhood, however—if we allow parenting to be the only thing that gives us a sense of purpose—then we are putting way too much psychological pressure on our children and ourselves.

Encouraging dependency after a child has developmentally outgrown the need can cause emotional difficulties and conflicts for children and within families. Part of motherhood is allowing our children the space and room to grow, separate, and individuate—that's a powerful gift.

We moms have to think every day about how to teach children about living so they can wisely and safely leave the nest. Doing everything for them isn't a part of this. This helping and giving instinct can sometimes be a way of feeding our own need to be needed. Giveaway Moms have to be always aware of this line and gently question themselves on their deeper motivations. This is so loving and helpful for kids and moms.

There is a fine line between loving and caring for our kids and living through them. Don't let yourself cross that line.

ALLOWING UNEARNED GUILT TO BE YOUR GUIDE

A friend and I went to the park with our children one day. It was cold outside, and she was trying to force a hat onto her two-year-old's head—but her daughter was screaming and running away from her. "Honey, I know you hate this," she said, "but it's mom disease. You know I can't help it—I've gotta put this hat on you!"

"What's 'mom disease'?" I asked her when the hat crisis was over and the kids were busy playing.

"Oh, you know what I mean," she said. "It's all the guilt we feel as mothers: the guilt when we don't feel like we are doing a good enough job taking care of our kids. The guilt we feel about wanting to escape some days. We feel guilty about taking a day off to do indulgent things and leave our children— then we feel bad because we're not taking care of ourselves. You know, mom disease."

I do know about mom disease, and you probably do, too, but much (if not all) of the guilt we feel as moms is unearned; it's largely a reaction to not being able to meet the unrealistic expectations we have for ourselves—a misplaced sense of having failed in some way.

Guilt is not *always* unearned, of course. As a clinical social worker, I've worked with battered, abused, and neglected children. I have seen firsthand the damage that parents can do when they don't feel guilty enough about not providing the care their children need. But these are extreme cases that fall on the other side of the spectrum from you, Giveaway Mom. Those parents give too little and don't feel guilty about it. You, meanwhile, are probably giving too much and still feel guilty for not giving more!

This guilt is not restricted to just one type of mother, either. Stay-at-home moms feel guilty for not bringing home a paycheck. Working moms feel guilty for being away from their kids when they're at work—and then they feel guilty for being away from work when they're with their kids. Single moms feel guilty for not having a partner, for raising their children in a "broken home," and the list goes on.

Start thinking about your mom guilt. What do you feel guilty about? When you think about it, do you really deserve that guilt? You probably don't. But until you figure how to move away from self-sacrifice and deal with your feelings of guilt, you're going to keep feeling bad about it anyway.

UNEARNED GUILT AS A MOTHER AND THE CODEPENDENT WAFFLE

Waffle as a verb means the inability to make a clear decision or know what to do. Many Giveaway Girls fall into this waffle pattern when they are parenting. They waffle in one of these three ways:

1. They are not good with their boundaries so they get manipulated by the "Oh, Mom, please..." emotional manipulation maneuvers. If you feel sorry for your kid due to divorce or some sort of disability or challenge, this can make the pleasing reaction even more prevalent for Giveaway Girl Moms. This is not good for you or your children! It stems from unearned guilt.

2. Giveaway Girl moms feel unearned guilt when they attempt to discipline their children, which leads them to be too permissive. Giveaway Girls have difficulty saying "no" and sticking to it. They feel like "making" their children feel bad is terrible so they can't set good limits. Wanting our children to be happy is a noble belief that often gets distorted in Giveaway Girl parenting.

3. Giveaway Girls can go from one extreme, being too permissive, to the other extreme, being too strict. "That's it. I am taking your cell phone for a week." Saying this after you ignored your child's breaking of the cellphone rules 20 times isn't really useful. When

you go all extreme in the other direction you aren't teaching, you are reacting to your own poor boundaries. This is a real easy Giveaway Girlism in motherhood.

Make sure you aren't going down these roads because you are too uncomfortable with your unearned guilt and boundaries.

PULLING THE WRONG HAIR: JUDGING OTHER WOMEN HARSHLY

Anne's husband kept sleeping with prostitutes. One day, Anne came home to find him at home in the middle of the day with yet another sex worker/prostitute. Understandably, Anne was quite upset, but instead of directing her anger at her husband, she was furious at the woman he was in bed with. She grabbed the woman by the ponytail, called her every vicious name in the book, and literally dragged her out the door by her hair.

Clearly, the ponytailed prostitute was not the problem; Anne's husband was. But her reaction—focusing her anger on the other woman in the room—is something that women, including mothers, do all the time. We tend to judge each other way more harshly than we judge men. Career moms, for example, can be very judgmental about stay-at-home moms ("Of course she had time to bake cookies—she doesn't have a real job"), while stay-at-home moms can be just as bad ("Why have children if they are just going to be raised by nannies?"). It happens a lot.

Kelly is a career mom, and it's obvious to everyone how little her husband is involved in the care of his children. When their son has a football game, Kelly's husband is nowhere to be found. He doesn't go to parent-teacher conferences. He interacts with the kids only when he feels like it. He has no time to "help" Kelly with any of "her" responsibilities. "That's just Ken," Kelly laughs, shrugging. "He'll never change."

Kelly never gets mad at her husband for leaving her to take care of everything—but she is the first to get mad at other moms. "Why didn't Anne invite Johnny to the playdate? She is such a bitch!" "Where the hell is Catherine with that birthday cake? I am so pissed!"

Don't be like Kelly, Giveaway Moms—don't blame the wrong person and put your energies where they don't belong. We are all in this together. Instead of tearing each other down, let's lean toward and support one another. Research shows that girlfriends have a huge impact on our ability to do well, feel well, and even live longer. So let's stop pulling the wrong hair.[7]

MOTHER BACKLASH: THE CONSEQUENCES OF BEING A GIVEAWAY MOM

Mother backlash happens when the pressure created by too much detrimental caretaking builds too high. At a certain point, Giveaway Moms give too much away—and then they break.

Sometimes this looks like a midlife crisis. Often it looks like a divorce, an addiction, or an affair. It can result in emotional shutdown; some mothers become so overwhelmed and depleted that they disconnect and are no longer mentally present in their relationship with their kids or partner. However it manifests, backlash is an inevitable result of the emotional impoverishment created by giving it away—and it's devastating for all involved.

Amy is a perfect example of mother backlash. She was married for twenty years and had four kids with her husband—a workaholic who left her with all of the responsibilities at home. She gave and gave . . . and then she met a man who told her how wonderful she was (something she hadn't heard from her husband in a long time). She divorced her husband, moved away from her kids ("I think I will parent in a different way from now on," she announced), and moved in with her boyfriend. It was too late for Amy to find balance within the context of raising her kids and within her marriage; she had given so much that she felt she had nothing left—so she left.

Detrimental caretaking to the point of backlash is common, and it's a danger to all Giveaway Moms out there. Your backlash might not be quite as intense as Amy's was, but if you're giving too much away, it will eventually happen, unless you make some serious changes.

SMART Parenting

Making a decision no longer to parent from a detrimentally caretaking place is SMART—which also happens to be the acronym for a parenting approach that you can use to create balance in your life. Not all parenting decisions can be made based on this formula, of course; it will, however, send you in the right direction.

S: Social and Self-Awareness

We are all a conglomeration of our biology, emotions, early childhood experiences, traumas, and strengths. Giveaway Moms often give too much because they suffered from their own needs not getting met as children, which can mean that many of their own issues are triggered by parenting their children—and this can be a slippery slope. It's important to be aware of your emotional "stuff" so you don't fall into the trap of parenting yourself through parenting your kids.

Great rewards come from gaining insight into your own inner workings.

It's equally important to be aware of the societal messages that might be influencing your decisions. Take back that power; your decision making needs to be clean. When you start feeling that mom guilt, or when you're anxious or confused about something, check in with yourself and ask yourself why you're feeling that way—whether it's for good reason or simply because you're trying to live up to unrealistic societal pressures.

Know your stuff so your kids can know theirs!

M: MONITOR YOUR ACTIONS AND MAKE CHANGES AS NEEDED

Ask yourself if you have a tendency to give it away in your mothering. Check in with yourself daily about whether you're engaging in detrimental caretaking—or find someone else to check in with about it.

Finding another mom on whom you can rely for support and accountability can be incredibly helpful. My closest friend and I, for example, call and leave each other voice mails when we catch ourselves detrimentally caretaking. We laugh at ourselves, encourage each other, and share with each other when we learn something new.

Do you do the codependent waffle? Once you start noticing your detrimental caretaking tendencies, start setting better boundaries. You don't have to go all extreme and shake up the whole household; think about it more like you're rearranging the furniture a little.

Make a simple change, like having your twelve-year-old do his laundry one weekend, then see how you feel afterward. Get more help. Delegate. Drop the ball a little so others can pick it up. You want to exercise? Say no to picking up your son from football practice if he can walk home, or see if he can ride home with someone else. Take small steps.

A: ATTACHMENT

Any good therapist will tell you that your emotional and physical attachment is the most important aspect of your relationship with your children. To value them is to love them, engage with them, spend time with them, and help them manage the complexities of life.

That doesn't mean you have to make sure they are happy with you all the time, Giveaway Moms; it simply means that it's important to be aware of what is going on emotionally with your kids. Check in with them about how they're feeling. Be present for them.

You don't have to coddle your children or make them feel better all the time—but you do need to be tuned in to their real emotional needs, especially when life gets busy. Listen to them; validate their difficulties with empathic words: "That sounds so frustrating, Kim."

R: REDUCE YOUR WORKLOAD

Remember the Swedish museum? Don't make the freaking homemade applesauce every day. Buy dessert for that dinner party, instead of making pie from scratch. When it comes to housework, focus on keeping two rooms clean, rather than the whole house.

To help you with this, I have invented the DEF (Daily Ease of Functioning) scale—a tool that I recommend you use in all of your decision making:

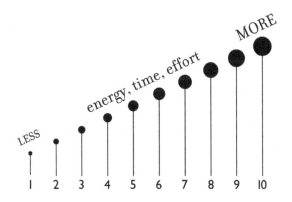

This scale may seem basic—but everything in life can be based on it. A score of 1 means that the amount of energy, effort, and time required is pretty minimal. A score of 10 represents the highest possible level of complication.

Everything you do each day falls somewhere on this scale; the only question is where. Which bank should you use? Which pants should you buy for your five-year-old? What should you serve your guests for dinner on Friday night? These are all questions that can be addressed using the DEF scale. Pick the bank that you're going to drive by all the time anyway, not the one across town. Buy the dark pants that aren't going to show stains you'll have to work to get rid of. Grill some flank steak, instead of trying out that complicated homemade sushi recipe for the first time. In other words, choose tasks with DEF scores of 1, 2, and 3 rather than 8, 9, and 10, whenever possible.

My friend Elaine uses the DEF strategy, and she says it's changed her life. "I've always planned these big, crazy birthday parties for Amelia," she told me recently, "but this year I decided to use the DEF scale. So I asked her where she wanted to have it, instead of assuming we would have it at my house—a DEF score of 10, when you think about cleaning the house before and after and protecting objects from destruction during—and she said she wanted it at Pump It Up."

Not only was Amelia's request within Elaine's budget, but having the party somewhere else meant that all she had to do was provide the dessert. Elaine used the DEF scale again when she was planning that—and it helped her settle on cupcakes, instead of cake. "Cupcakes are easier for kids to eat, and they don't require forks and plates. Plus, that way there was no leftover cake for me to eat, so I wouldn't regain the five pounds I had just lost from Christmas," Elaine explained. "I had so much fun—and it was such a breeze. You can't tell me that me having the party at my house and exhausting myself would have made my daughter any happier with her big day."

Not all decisions have to be made using the DEF scale, of course. Yes, maybe the school across the street is more convenient, but if it's not nearly as good as the school ten miles away, driving farther each day may feel worth it.

It's important to keep in mind the daily strains of the choices you make and to pick your battles accordingly. Too many moms feel guilty when they cut corners, when the truth is that there's nothing wrong with making your life less difficult! Do the extra work when you have to—but don't martyr yourself for stuff that really isn't that important.

T: TAKE CARE OF YOURSELF

How do you care for yourself? We will talk more about this in later chapters, but I recommend doing at least two things each day that are just for you. That might mean getting up ten minutes early to do some meditation. It might mean taking a fifteen-minute walk at lunch. It might even mean simply allotting five minutes at night to mentally go through your day and be compassionate and encouraging to yourself about what you accomplished—no ticking off what you did wrong, just celebrating the good stuff. For instance, you could tell yourself, *I like how you took time to have a cup of tea today. Very good.* Does that sound dumb? Maybe—but it sure feels good.

What have you been putting off about your self-care since you became a mom?

Another way to figure out what you may be missing is to fantasize about what you would do if you had the time? Do you ever think, *When the kids grow up, I'm going to start a cooking class?* These fantasies or ideas are actually what you may need right now. Deflecting and putting these things off could be a form of unnecessary self-sacrifice.

If you do nothing else that I recommend in this whole book, start doing two things every day to take care of yourself. It is impossible to make positive changes in your life with an empty gas tank. Once you start taking better care of yourself, everything else will get better, too. Go ahead—try it and see.

FINDING A BALANCE

Overwhelmed by the idea of making so many changes to the way you do things? Remember, there's no need to do it all today. Go slow and easy. We want progress, not perfection. And just reading this book is a huge step forward.

Feel free to wait until you've finished reading this book before you start making active changes. If you feel ready, you may want to start making a list—in your head or anywhere else —of ways in which you may be engaging in detrimental caretaking as a mom, and post a little note somewhere to remind yourself that you don't have to do it all. For now, though, it's enough that the wheels have begun turning and you are starting to see yourself and your world differently.

A healthy balance between loving others and showing love and compassion to yourself is paramount to good child rearing. You may not be where you want to be yet, Giveaway Mom—but you are on your way!

I have never experienced so much joy as I did when I became a mom. I am privileged and honored. It is definitely the best thing and the hardest thing I have ever done. In addition, I adore the caring and nurturing part and being there for my family. However, this role has to encompass self-nurturing, and we mothers have to be vigilant at addressing our emotional integrity throughout this process, no matter what society "tells" us.

⌒

CHAPTER 4

GIVEAWAY WIVES AND GIRLFRIENDS

"The things that we love tell us what we are."
—THOMAS AQUINAS

All healthy intimate relationships require give-and-take. In the throes of romance and love, this giving comes easily; after all, being in love and caring deeply for someone is one of the most pleasurable experiences life has to offer. For Giveaway Girls, however, the intimate-partner role can be a treacherous one. Giveaway Girls already tend to give too much of themselves to others—so when they add love to the equation, they create an environment ripe for all kinds of detrimental caretaking.

- How do you decide what is detrimental caretaking in your intimate relationships and what is not?
- How do you know if your partnership is healthy?
- What kinds of partners are dangerous to Giveaway Girls?
- How do you build a partnership that meets your needs when you're not used to meeting them yourself?

◦ Are you listening to what society is telling you about your relationships (or lack thereof), instead of listening to yourself?

These are questions that all Giveaway Girls should ask themselves, because most of them struggle with detrimental caretaking in their intimate relationships. They do it when they're dating; they do it with the people they are already in relationships with. It's a dangerous, slippery slope.

This chapter covers some issues that Giveaway Girls face in their intimate relationships. It offers tips about what to avoid—including certain types whom Giveaway Girls tend to be attracted to (but who are terrible for them), unhealthy beliefs about relationships, and how changing your mind can change your life.

Take mental notes and be brave here, Giveaway Girl. It's so important to your well-being that you shine a light on the places in your intimate relationships where you might be detrimentally caretaking. It may make you uncomfortable to see just how many ways you're giving it away—but hey, it's exciting to see what you can change to improve things, too! Let's start by taking a look at unequal partnerships.

EIGHT TYPES OF UNEQUAL PARTNERSHIPS

When it comes to women's experiences with marriage, the statistics aren't pretty—in fact, studies have shown that women are less happy in their marriages than men, are more likely than men to see problems in their marriages, are more likely to initiate divorce (they ask for divorce two-thirds of the time), and are less likely to say that they want to marry again after having been married before than are men who have been married before.[1],[2]

How many times have you seen an incredible woman in your life hook herself up to someone who is really not her equal? Who takes advantage of her? Who doesn't treat her well? It happens a lot—but it doesn't need to happen to you. The first step in keeping yourself out of an unequal partnership is learning what types of people to avoid getting into a relationship with in the first place. Or, if you find yourself already in one of these relationships, adopt some Got It Girl strategies to shift this dynamic into a healthier balance. We will get to those later in the book!

To help you out at identifying these guys, here are the eight most common types that Giveaway Girls fall for—to their detriment, of course.

BOXCAR WILLIES

The name Boxcar Willie is a historical reference to men who lived in boxcars (the freight cars of trains) during the Great Depression, when times were tough in the United States and unemployment hit an all-time high. Some of the thousands of men who had nowhere to live after they lost their jobs began hopping on boxcars and riding from one town to the next, begging or doing odd jobs for cash. Today, though, those men who in the past might've ridden the rails now just hitch up with successful women who support them financially. It's a trend I like to call the Boxcar Willie Phenomenon, and it's more common than you might think, now that so many women out there are making incomes large enough to support themselves and others. It even happens to the women who don't have big incomes too.

It's often difficult to spot today's Willies, however, because they don't ride around in boxcars anymore; they lease cars on shaky credit (or they figure out a way to get their girlfriends/ wives to pay for them). And instead of dining on baked beans around a campsite, they might even be foodies who frequently "forget" their wallet or plead that they're "having a tough time right now" when the bill comes. Maybe their meanie ex has them cash strapped "temporarily." So what does the Giveaway Girl do? She picks up the check.

Linda met Joe when she was working full-time as an office assistant at a Fortune 500 company. Joe was handsome, in his thirties. Linda and he shared similar political views and ambitions. Joe had a scattered work history but claimed it was because he hadn't found his calling yet.

When they got married, Joe immediately quit his job and signed up for graduate school. Linda supported him. Then Joe quit grad school too. He couldn't handle getting another job. Linda was there for him with that as well, emotionally and financially supporting him wholeheartedly. Meanwhile, with kids soon in the picture, Linda earned promotion after promotion, until she eventually became a partner at her company and was making a seven-figure income.

Joe spent all his time on the computer most days; he didn't clean or do anything to help run the house, and he didn't help with the kids. But he did encourage Linda and tell her how proud of her he was. Linda felt torn: On the one hand, Joe seemed supportive, but on the other hand, she didn't believe she could depend on him in any way, and that didn't feel very good.

> *There is absolutely nothing wrong with partner-*
> *ships in which only one person brings home money, of*
> *course. But both parties need to respect each other and*
> *agree that both will contribute equally to sustain the*
> *relationship. If each person is satisfied that the other is*
> *doing his or her fair share to make things work, then*
> *that's one thing. But if something else is going on . . .*
> *well, then something else is going on.*
>
> ↪

LAME-DUCK PARTNERS

Lame ducks are guys who don't do anything to help around the house or work to sustain their partnerships. They may have gainful employment, but they are self-centered and always have a "What about me?" mentality when making decisions—even decisions that will affect their partners. These are the guys whose golf game comes before anything else. Some of these partners aren't mean about it and don't appear selfish, but they still aren't stepping up to equally participate in the relationship.

Some lame ducks can get that they aren't pulling their weight if you explain your chronic dissatisfaction to them. However, a true lame-duck partner will not make changes, even with couples' counseling, no matter how many times he says he will. A few are simply incorrigible no matter what you do.

ADDICTS

Depending on the research that you look at, some statistics conclude that as many as 23.5 million Americans are addicted to alcohol or drugs—in other words, one in every ten people. [3] And this figure doesn't even take into account other addictions (sex, gambling, debt, porn, etc.).

Being with an addict is horribly difficult and traumatizing. Unfortunately, many Giveaway Girls are susceptible to getting involved in these types of relationships. The disease of addiction draws out detrimental caretaking tendencies.

The addict "needs" so much attention, worry, and energy, and so upsets the world, that a Giveaway Girl can't even begin to think about what she needs for herself. Once she has connected with this type of partner, it is extremely difficult for a Giveaway Girl to be healthy. Luckily, there are twelve-step and other counseling programs available for those who are in this situation—but in order to seek out help, you first have to recognize there's a problem.

ABUSERS

Abusers are people who get what they want when they want it through physical and/or verbal intimidation and abuse. They don't compromise, listen to others' needs, work on growing as a person, or give as well as receive—instead, they use bullying as a short path to getting what they want.

Giveaway Girls are especially prone to falling for verbal abusers because they tend to accept the abusers' opinions and start to self-doubt. This makes them susceptible to others' control and more likely to internalize put-downs and criticisms. This, in turn, makes the Giveaway Girl feel more and more powerless and weak.

Some favorite tactics verbal abusers use:

- They criticize or put you down.
- They usurp your confidence.

- ❧ They shame or embarrass you.
- ❧ They try to make you feel like you are not smart or can't do things.
- ❧ They confuse you ("Are you sure you want to do that?").
- ❧ They start isolating you from friends and family.

I feel great sympathy for women who love abusers. It's hard to turn away from someone you love because they can't stop hurting you—and it's especially hard for Giveaway Girls, who can always see the good in others. (Hey, everyone can have positive qualities.) If you're in an abusive relationship, Giveaway Girl—whether the abuse is physical or verbal—it's imperative that you get help and support outside the relationship if you truly want to be happy and healthy.

MEAT BOSSES

These guys have to have things their way. They may not be as aggressive as abusers, but somehow they always manage to be the ones making the rules. I use the term "meat boss" to describe this type because one guy I met who fit this profile insisted on being in charge of the cooking, and he liked to make only really fattening stuff (heavy Italian sausages, steaks, hamburgers with duck-fat fries). His wife told me she hated eating such greasy, fatty food all the time, but she didn't want to hurt his feelings by complaining.

Meat Boss was in charge of more than just the kitchen—he made all the financial decisions, too. His wife didn't even know where he kept their checkbook. (*T-r-o-u-b-l-e.*) Anytime she tried to bring up her concerns, he freaked out, so she thought it was easier just to go along with him, even if she was unhappy.

ONE-FOOT-OUT GUYS

The one-foot-out guy is a great guy—everything a girl could ever want. Only problem is, he just can't commit to anything more serious. He wants to, but the time just isn't right—"yet."

Many a wonderful Giveaway Girl has spent years of her life hitched to a guy who will never move forward with her. And it sucks—even more so because these guys seem perfect on the surface. They aren't mean, they're tons of fun, they appear to really have their stuff together, and they seem to be going places with their life. But the words "Let's move this relationship forward—now" will never issue from their lips.

Granted, not all Giveaway Girls want to take things to a more intimate level or get married. But for those who do, this is a tough place to be for both parties, and it's hard knowing when to walk away.

Amanda dated a married man for several years, despite her wanting a commitment. He promised he'd leave his wife for her (they were having so much trouble, he said). As time went on, the split never happened, but Amanda stayed with him anyway—the Giveaway Girl on the side, waiting and letting her blind love and optimism compromise her judgment and good sense. I wonder if Amanda is still waiting. That's a tough spot to be in.

CHEATERS

Cheater types can sometimes be identified by their wandering eyes. This happens when the cheater you're on a date with gets distracted by a passing person of interest.

A cheater cannot stay focused on his partner without having someone on the side. Maybe he is a sex addict who hides from his feelings, or maybe he just chooses this life because of the excitement.

Regardless of the intent, trusting, loving, incredible women have fallen in love with partners like this since the beginning of time. Keep your eyes open, ladies.

CONTROLLERS

Controllers usually sweep you off your feet in no time. They quickly figure out how to be your Prince Charming. Soon after you are hooked, they start asking you to make some changes. These might include not wearing as much makeup or not being on Facebook "because of all the competitive guy attention" you are getting. Controllers are jealous of innocent behavior.

A controlling partner might say something like, "For your own good, you need to ...." This person usually isn't crazy about your having close friends or family members because he has a strong need to control, and smart controllers know that support is the gateway to your freedom to live a happy, balanced life.

Watch out, Giveaway Girl—what feels at first like caring and love can soon take away your power.

THE COMMON LINK: NARCISSISM AND/OR EMOTIONAL MANIPULATORS

As you may have noticed, the eight types we just discussed have something in common: they each display more than a little narcissism in their behaviors. There is little give-and-take in relationships with men like these. They are extremely self-focused, they lack empathy, and their primary objective is always for their needs be met first. And this makes sense, because Giveaway Girls tend toward the opposite end of this spectrum, putting others' needs before their own—which, of course, for a narcissist is a very attractive proposition.

It makes sense that a narcissist would want to date someone who wants to take care of him. But why are narcissistic men so compelling to Giveaway Girls? Well, for one, they appear to have what many Giveaway Girls lack: where a Giveaway Girl may have trouble with self-confidence, the narcissistic guy (NG) appears and behaves confidently. Where a Giveaway Girl may not always know exactly what to do, the NG always acts like he does. Where a Giveaway Girl might be reluctant to ask her partner to meet her needs, the NG makes sure his needs get met. And this can be very seductive for some Giveaway Girls.

Even after it becomes clear that the qualities she first found attractive in her partner are actually symptoms of a less-than-desirable personality, it can be incredibly difficult for the Giveaway Girl to break free of the relationship. Why? Because she tends to be loyal and loving, to see the best in others, and to feel the need to caretake and sacrifice. In essence, these women are not only able but also willing to tolerate the intolerable—and that keeps them from leaving relationships that aren't good for them.

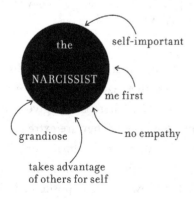

These unequal relationships can be incredibly destructive for Giveaway Girls, because narcissistic partners offer little, if any, reciprocity in their relationships. A Giveaway Girl who falls for an emotional unequal is bound for a lot of resentment and frustration down the line because of the inequality in that partnership.

James Fogarty, a specialist on emotional manipulators, writes that the following qualities make people more vulnerable to emotional manipulators:

- Codependent
- Looking for love—desperately
- Caring and loving
- Want to please/feel overly responsible
- Unfulfilled needs
- Abuse or neglected in childhood
- Vulnerable
- Immune to falling out of love

It is important to remember as you look at the above illustration that women are not only the caretakers in this dynamic. There are narcissistic women out there too! It is applicable to both genders. In fact, there are many wonderful, caring, and smart men who end up falling for narcissistic women.

When Giveaway Girls date or marry these guys, they may not have a clue how their prospective partner will pick up on these characteristics. But it's that very lack of awareness that makes them such easy prey to intentional emotional manipulators. Yet in many instances, that manipulation is so subtle, you can't perceive it. The partner is used to getting his way and having his love interests go along with his line of thinking and behaving. If he's manipulative, he may not know it or seem malicious about it. It just comes naturally.

Intentional or not, the outcome is the same.

WHAT PUTS US AT RISK OF FORMING UNEQUAL PARTNERSHIPS?

In Chapter 2, we covered a wide range of unhealthy beliefs that cater to the detrimental caretaking lifestyle. These ways of thinking get Giveaway Girls into deep trouble.

Again, Giveaway Girl, it isn't your fault. A lot of what we decide to do as individuals has to do with these beliefs and what we understand our role to be. We unconsciously accept messages that tell us what to do and not to do in life—messages like "you're less valuable if you're not in a relationship," and "it's a woman's job to be a caregiver"—and that acceptance naturally sets us up for unhealthy and dysfunctional relationship beliefs. Yes, these messages are still present, despite how evolved we are, and over time, the messages morph into unhealthy beliefs that I'll explain one by one. It's so important for you to change your mind about these.

UNHEALTHY BELIEFS

- Words are as important as actions.
- Love is all about sacrifice and giving . . . even if I'm the only one doing it.
- Predictability is boring.
- I shouldn't have to ask my partner to fulfill my needs. He should just know by now that I need ....
- If I have to ask for what I need, it doesn't count.

- If I don't ...., he will leave and I will be alone forever.
- If I ignore our problems, there won't be any problems.
- If I go along with what he wants, it will just be easier.
- If .... changes, I will be happy.
- I just need to adjust to how things are, even if I am unhappy, because adjusting is better than the alternative.

How to Change Your Mind

Unhealthy Belief #1

Words are as important as actions.

As women, we love to hear nice things; we love to talk; we value what is being said. Studies have actually shown that verbal communication is far more important to women than it is to men. Because of this—and as any man can tell you—most women buy into way too much, way too early.

If you spot a behavior in your mate that annoys or disturbs you, pay attention to it, rather than making excuses for it. People tell you and show you exactly who they are by how they act—especially in stressful situations. "He is really sweet; he just didn't call because he got busy." Really? Or is it that he didn't call because other things are more important to him than standing by his word? Remember, dating someone is a lot like interviewing them for a job: any small red flags you see in your first couple of meetings can turn into huge irritations and issues once you've hired that person.

People *can* change. As a therapist, I have seen people reverse the destructive course of their life and learn new, healthy behaviors and attitudes. But the changes take consistent effort over time—and effort requires action. A silver tongue isn't enough to keep a relationship strong; if you want to ensure that your partnership is equal, use behavior, not words, as your barometer.

UNHEALTHY BELIEF #2

Love is all about sacrifice and giving . . .
even if I'm the only one doing it.

Sure, relationships require some sacrifice. But unequal sacrifice equals an unhealthy relationship, and it's a pattern that too many Giveaway Girls fall into.

I'm not saying you should abandon your loved one if he falls ill or gets seriously injured. Extraordinary circumstances may demand that, for a time, one person gives a little more of X or the other gives more of Y. Take my friend Geoff: When he went through a bout of mild depression, his wife picked up the slack and relieved him of many household responsibilities. He was grateful for her understanding and compassion, and he went to extraordinary lengths to get better so she wouldn't have to shoulder the burden for too long. When she went through her own, employment-related funk a few years later, Geoff stood behind her, adding to his plate of responsibilities to take some pressure off her.

So what is equitable? This is largely a matter of opinion—but what it comes down to is that whatever you do for your partner, it needs to come from a healthy place. If I gladly take care of my husband after a car accident, it should be because I love him; it shouldn't be because I'm making what I like to call a "shadow deal." (That means I have a secret expectation that if I give everything now, I will get something I want or need in return.)

If I make sacrifices for my partner from an unhealthy place —out of a feeling of powerlessness, not love—then my giving takes on a very different meaning, and I am engaging in detrimental caretaking.

Relationships are composed of give-and-take—not just "give."

When Shadow Deals Go Bad

Shadow deals are when Giveaway Girls think that if they sacrifice their needs for their partner, they will get something in return. Shadow deals occur behind the scenes, and they can be unconsciously made so that you don't even know you are thinking them. They're hidden expectations.

Tabitha worked two waitress jobs a day so her boyfriend could go to chiropractic school. She cleaned the house they shared, paid all their bills, and never asked him to contribute. She was happy to do it—because she believed that if their roles were reversed, he would do the same for her. She never asked him if that was the case, and he never said it was, but she felt secure in the knowledge that he was just as willing to sacrifice for her as she was for him.

Tabitha lived in Chicago, and all her family members—with whom she was very close—lived close by. But when her boyfriend said he wanted to move home to California and asked her to come with him, she did. And once there, she molded herself into his life. She went out with his friends. She hung out with his mother. And she thought she was happy . . . but over time, the relationship crumbled. She began to resent the time and energy her boyfriend spent hanging out with his friends, without a thought to prioritizing her, and they began to fight. Eventually, he broke up with her. Unhappy as she was, she couldn't bring herself to leave him. After her boyfriend ended things, Tabitha moved back to Chicago and spent the next six months crying in a dark, depressing studio apartment. By the time she came to see me, she was barely able to leave her place just to commute to work, all because she had ignored her self-care and failed to set boundaries. If she had talked things out with her boyfriend, instead of making a shadow deal with herself, maybe she would've discovered much earlier that he wasn't ready to reciprocate in the sacrifice department.

Tabitha could have scaled back a little—not to punish him, but to avoid setting herself up for disappointment and heartbreak.

～❧～

UNHEALTHY BELIEF #3

Predictability is boring.

Some Giveaway Girls think that a guy who calls when he says he is going to call, who is predictable and not full of games and drama, is a turn-off. They want danger, excitement, wham-bam-knock-you-off-your-feet chemistry. They want bad boys. And it almost always ends in heartache.

Let's be clear: liking the bad boys isn't the problem—dating and marrying them even though they treat you poorly is. That's not to say that chemistry isn't important, of course. I'm not advocating for the idea that you should settle for less just because a guy is safe and solvent. However, you shouldn't settle for less than what you deserve just because a guy is hot and rides a motorcycle, either.

"Unpredictable" is often just a nicer word for "narcissistic"—and you can't have a fulfilling relationship with someone who's interested only in his own needs.

UNHEALTHY BELIEF #4

I shouldn't have to ask my partner to fulfill my needs. He should just know by now that I need ....

Some women have a strong desire for their loved one to know or sense automatically what it is they need. They want a partner who is tuned into them and knows when they need reassurance, encouragement, even a kiss on the cheek.

For women who have these beliefs, they can feel like a deep longing, an emptiness, a loneliness inside, that they believe will be assuaged only by the nourishment of their partner's response. It is painful and hurtful for them when their partner doesn't just get it. *After all, aren't I worth it?* they think.

The reality is that these women don't want anything unreasonable; they would just like their partner to pay attention to them and give them what doesn't need saying. This need sometimes arises from a painful, primitive place. Not having that essential nurturing and caretaking in their primary years can create a painful void.

Having to ask for your needs can feel like it defeats exactly what it is you need: to be seen, to be cared for, to be acknowledged as worthy and lovable. You can unknowingly and under-standably put too much emphasis on this request and repeatedly end up feeling defeated and hurt when it cannot be met.

Ask and You Shall Receive

When Peggy first came to see me, she was furious with her husband. She felt invisible to him. He never seemed to notice or appreciate it when she did an excep-tionally good job of handling their kids, or when she made him a special gourmet dinner, or even when she threw him a beautiful party for his fortieth birthday. After years of feeling this way, Peggy had built up resentment and often found herself making sarcastic statements to others about her husband.

Through our work, Peggy and I discovered that she had no good relationship model upon which to base her marriage. Her parents had both been alcoholics, and she had been extremely emotionally neglected as a child—something that explained why she wanted so desperately to be "seen" by her husband. Asking for what she needed didn't feel like love to her.

Eventually, Peggy began asking for what she needed—and then she started receiving it. It took a while for her emotions to catch up with that deep-rooted need not to have to ask, so it felt a little fake at first. But once she allowed herself time and practice, her feelings caught up and her relationship with her husband hugely improved. He'd been willing to give her what she needed all along; all she had to do was ask!

UNHEALTHY BELIEF #5

If I have to ask for what I need, it doesn't count.

Asking for what you need from a partner with specifics, and in many different ways (sometimes many times), is part of a healthy partnership. Unfortunately, Giveaway Girls tend to sacrifice their needs so often that when they know the one thing they really need, so much emotional energy rides on it that if their partner falls short, the explosion can be way out of proportion with the issue at hand: *Did my partner give only because I asked? He didn't really want to do it in the first place! It doesn't count. It doesn't count!*

Consider instead that a lot of times someone doesn't know what you need until you ask. If they did, that would be mind reading, and most people can't read minds. That's why we should always have the courage to speak up. Then, when our requests repeatedly go unmet or ignored, and conflict or, worse, aggression arises, we need help.

With some partners, you have to ask repeatedly, sometimes within the context of marital counseling, to consistently get what you need. As a marital counselor, I often see that one partner keeps giving their partner what they think their partner wants, not what their partner is asking them. Very frustrating. Don't give up too soon.

It will be true for some, unfortunately, that a partner will not give. The most important part here is trying for yourself in the right way—speak up, speak clearly, be specific.

Remember, within the asking is the gracious act of caring for and nurturing your being. Even if you don't get exactly the results you want, you were direct and honest, which is a gift in itself.

UNHEALTHY BELIEF #6

If I don't ...., he will leave and I will be alone forever.

We all need and crave human connection—but for some, this motivating force is greater than it is for others. Women have been culturally indoctrinated to believe that they "need" coupledom. Just ask any single gal over the age of thirty if she feels any pressure to get married, or at least to be coupled up with someone. Whether or not she buys into the idea, that pressure is there—and it can make some Giveaway Girls sacrifice more than they would like to in the name of not ending up alone.

If fear is driving the choices you make in your relationship, it's time to rethink things. Just as your decisions shouldn't come from a place of powerlessness, they shouldn't come from a place of anxiety, either.

Having a trusted counselor is a wonderful way to work on the powerful fears and anxieties that put us on paths we really don't want in our life.

UNHEALTHY BELIEF #7

If I ignore our problems, there won't be any problems.

Denial is subconscious and powerful. We deny things when we are feeling powerless and incapable of resolving them. Denial is also a helpful defense against overwhelmingly negative emotions and circumstances. Sometimes our minds just say no to what is happening. This happens a lot to women in relationships with partners who are addicted or abusive in any way.

Denial serves its purpose in extreme situations—but you can't stay there forever. Taking good care of you includes learning how to live in denial no longer. Face up to the things that are really bothering you.

UNHEALTHY BELIEF #8

If I go along with what he wants,
it will just be easier.

This is the most common unhealthy belief among all the women I know, including me. I know so many women who get stuck in this trap. They think that if you do what their partner wants and just go along with it, then they can avoid the fight, avoid the discomfort or the negative feelings—that it will be worth it.

I totally do this sometimes and I HAVE to catch myself. This is dangerous in terms of personal boundaries. Whenever you downplay your needs and don't set boundaries, you will eventually leak gas out of your tank and negatively affect your life.

It may seem easier to go along, but that is an erroneous and unhealthy belief. What happens when, later on, you are feeling overwhelmed, annoyed, and resentful? Codependent depressive rage (explained at the end of this chapter) happens. Stop this belief and replace it with a careful reevaluation of your boundaries, which we will cover more fully in Chapter 8.

UNHEALTHY BELIEF #9

If .... changes, I will be happy.

This happens a lot when a partner has an addiction or an alcohol problem or there is a repeated issue that you feel is driving you nuts. Thoughts run like this:

- If he would just stop drinking too much, I would be happy.
- If he would just start making our family a priority, I would be happy.
- If he would just not be so tight with his money, I would be happy.
- If he would just not always want to go out with his friends and make me a priority, I would be happy.

It is amazing what kind of joy and gratefulness you can find in life even if your partner has really annoying behaviors or characteristics. In some relationships, you must leave because the issues are too dark and damaging to stay. However, sometimes you can find freedom in and appreciation of the relationship by adjusting your worldview and making changes in your self-care. The way you live can make a difficult situation much better.

If your loved one has an addiction, you may want to try being active in a twelve-step group, or at least get counseling. This could help you figure out things from a power-based worldview, versus giving the other person all the power to "make" you happy or unhappy.

Unhealthy Belief #10

I just need to adjust to how things are, even if I am unhappy, because adjusting is better than the alternative.

If you are in this mindset, then you are definitely being led by fear, anxiety, or an inaccurate sense of powerlessness. Yes, sometimes adjusting to how things are is useful. However, too many Giveaway Girls accept things that aren't okay because they feel like there is no fix.

For example, Betty had been married for twenty-five years to a man who was a workaholic. He would never go on vacation, he would never make time to attend kids' events, he would never make an effort to go on a date or to spend time with Betty. She accepted this but was miserable. Finally, she decided she wasn't going to put up with it anymore. She started planning trips with her kids, going out with her friends, taking classes, and doing more fulfilling things. Interestingly, her husband, Bob, then started finding time for her and the kids, and the relationship turned around. The funny thing is, Betty had figured out how to make herself happy and fulfilled in the context of this difficulty. Instead of accepting it in a powerless, sad way, she used her energy to make good things happen for herself, changed her perspective, and thus changed the dynamic of her marriage.

Clearly, things could have continued as they were with Bob, and eventually Betty might have discovered a different partner or even that she would like to be by herself. You never know how things will turn out in the long run, but when you make a consistent effort to make yourself happy and care for your needs where you can, good things eventually turn up.

SIGNS TO LOOK OUT FOR

You have every right to expect certain things from a partner—things that many Giveaway Girls don't demand for themselves.

A great way to build a relationship that meets your needs is to start out with a partner who isn't coming into your life with already-formed bad habits. Here are some red flags to keep an eye out for:

- He's always justifying how his way is "better."
- When you ask for something you want, he uses words like "selfish" or "unreasonable" or implies that your request is one of those things.
- He thinks mostly about what he wants and tends to put himself first.
- He is reluctant to take any responsibility for himself in disagreements—nothing is ever his fault.
- He doesn't follow through on his word consistently.

Sometimes these signs simply aren't there at the beginning. It happens. More often, though, they are there but we ignore them because we're so excited to be in a relationship. That's totally understandable. Unfortunately, this denial makes things more difficult later on.

Most Giveaway Girls who end up in an unequal partnership slink into acceptance of the imbalance without putting up a fight—until they just can't take anymore and things come to a head.

DETRIMENTAL CARETAKING AND BACKLASH

Just to review, here are a few ways in which Giveaway Girls tend to detrimentally caretake in their relationships:

- They don't ask for their partner to meet their needs.

- They think that by tolerating difficult (or even unacceptable) behaviors, they are being nice to and caring about their partner.

- They often feel hurt but don't feel like they can tell their partner, for fear of coming off as too needy or oversensitive.

- They deny to themselves the depth of their discomfort and dissatisfaction.

- They stuff down their feelings, setting themselves up for resentment and, in extreme circumstances, codependent depressive rage.

- They give too much power to their partner without even realizing it.

CODEPENDENT DEPRESSIVE RAGE

The vast majority of Giveaway Girls I work with don't make it into the therapist's office until they are struggling with what I call codependent depressive rage (CDR): an overwhelming feeling of depression or anger that stems from a buildup of resentment over unmet needs.

CDR isn't restricted to intimate relationships, of course—overgiving in any area of your life will eventually lead to a backlash. And when the resentment gets to this point, it is sometimes irreversible. Once a partner moves past CDR and into not caring about the relationship anymore, it feels almost unfixable—they are just done.

The worst part about CDR is that it is preventable. Most Giveaway Girls don't address their needs, because they are afraid of harming their relationship, but the truth is, taking care of yourself, not letting resentments fester and build, and daring to state your needs is what will save your relationship. Detrimental caretaking and ignoring your feelings, on the other hand, are surefire ways to corrode your relationship from the inside out.

I had always assumed that the word "backlash" had something to do with a whip, but when I looked it up a few years ago, I was surprised to learn that it actually has to do with machinery. Put a mechanical device under too much pressure, and it will eventually produce an undesirable, unintended misfire that can result in reversed energy and serious damage—something like a rubber band on an overstretched slingshot snapping and hurting the person who uses it.

This is exactly what happens with Giveaway Girl backlash: over time, resentment builds and builds, and eventually so much pressure accumulates that it has to be released. When this happens, the Giveaway Girl either explodes, lashing out at the people around her, or implodes, collapsing into a black hole of CDR.

Many Good Men

There are so many wonderful guys out there who would and do make incredible partners. In fact, the eight examples I listed are extremes and definitely the minority.

So what makes up a great guy anyway? Does the ideal man exist?

I think that looking for the PERFECT guy is like looking for the perfect home. It doesn't exist. Men and women alike have their good and not-so-good attributes. Even the best have bad days once in a while. However, the good men I know show the following characteristics:

- *They are loving, caring, and compassionate.*
- *They don't need to control you or anything else.*
- *They express themselves respectfully.*
- *They are good listeners.*
- *They admire and respect their partner.*
- *They keep their word and follow through.*
- *They take care of themselves while balancing the needs of those around them.*
- *They share responsibilities with their partner.*
- *They spend time with their kids.*
- *They have insight into their emotional life, and they work on this to continue learning and growing.*
- *They make decisions based on the principles of their highest self.*
- *When they have challenges, they work through them. When wrong, they admit it, make amends and try to do it differently next time.*
- *They are open-hearted, supportive, encouraging and positive.*

A healthy relationship is one in which you are free to be and think independently, to live without walking on eggshells or, worse, in fear. A healthy relationship is not without challenges, but the core condition of the healthy relationship revolves around personal freedom, mutual respect and admiration, and feeling supported and encouraged.

❦

The first time you take on too much for your partner or enable his dysfunctional behavior, you unwittingly set a wave into motion. That wave starts out small, but every time you "give it away" on your partner's behalf, it grows—getting bigger, heavier, and faster—until it brandishes a menacing momentum all its own. If you still the waters soon enough, you can avoid disaster, but if you let it build to tsunami-level force, it very well may drown you and everyone around you.

IS YOUR PARTNERSHIP EQUAL? QUESTIONS TO ASK YOURSELF

- Am I getting what I am giving overall?
- Am I being treated with respect and consideration?
- Does my partner try to see where I am coming from?
- Do I have equal power in decision making?
- Can I feel safe and confident sharing my opinions?
- How do we handle our disagreements?
- Do we complement each other and bring out the best in each other—or do we bring out each other's worst?

EIGHT HABITS FOR HEALTHIER RELATIONSHIPS

Whether or not you are currently in a relationship, the following action steps can make a big difference in your life, Giveaway Girl. Do these things in all of your relationships, and you will be ready to implement them in your intimate life as well. You can use these action items as reflection points: Which areas did you have trouble with in your past relationships, and how can you do things differently in the future to avoid having trouble with those same issues again?

ASK FOR WHAT YOU WANT.

You will probably feel very uncomfortable when you first begin asking your partner to meet your needs. You may also feel extremely guilty, but rest assured, this is unearned, BS guilt that comes from deep, dark, and entirely un-useful places. Ask for what you want. Be specific. Push through your discomfort, and you'll discover a whole new world on the other side.

IDENTIFY YOUR FEARS SO THEY DON'T TAKE OVER.

Fear can be huge—but it is rarely helpful. If you're operating from a place of fear in your relationship, try talking to your fears (no, I'm not kidding) or writing them out. Another good tactic is to blurt out three things that you are afraid of as loudly as you can (I suggest doing this in a car or some other place where you are alone) when you're feeling anxious. Make sure you check in with yourself often to see what fears are lurking. Are you afraid of being alone? Afraid of looking stupid? Afraid of disappointing your loved ones? We are all afraid of something. The trick is to keep that fear from controlling us.

TAKE BETTER CARE OF YOURSELF.

Self-care is an essential item on this list. Unfortunately, however, I've found that many Giveaway Girls are turned off by the concept of self-care—probably because for women who love to take care of everyone else, focusing on taking care of themselves feels wrong. The problem is, a woman who is not tending to herself is unlikely to have the self-esteem, strength, and awareness to implement positive changes in her life. And it's not just about you—one study I stumbled upon years ago asserted that married women who take care of themselves are 200 percent more likely to stay married (a win for everyone involved!). Now, I do not know if that was a real study, but I suspect there's some great truth therein. So try putting yourself first—just for a while—and see how it feels. Who knows—you might like it!

Here's an example of a Giveaway Girl named Adra and her husband Alf that I shared about on my blog at www.stopgivingitaway.com. See how Adra's taking care of herself changed the relationship...

ADRA - THE GIVEAWAY GIRL

Adra is married to Alf, a blend of the aforementioned types. Her husband doesn't do anything to help around the house. He comes in and turns on the TV or goes out with his friends. He makes fun of the 20 pounds she has gained in the last 10 years. When he does this, she just grimaces or offers a weak, "Cut it out."

Adra often does everything herself at home, despite having kids old enough to take on some responsibility. She talks to herself in really demeaning and negative ways too. "Why am I so tired? Why do I say such stupid things? What is wrong with me that my husband treats me this way?" Alf drinks too much too. He often wonders how he got stuck with such a lousy, nagging wife.

THE NEW ADRA – A GOT IT GIRL

Adra is enjoying her life so much better. She gets up early now to take walks, read her meditations, and prepares a healthy lunch for herself. She started requesting family meetings, and even though her husband refused to attend, she and the kids worked out an agreement for them to take more house responsibilities. Adra made sure to assign jobs to Alf (since he refused to discuss these issues).

Adra knows that Alf will intentionally botch the jobs (helplessness as manipulation) so she refused to set herself up to be resentful. She picked jobs that would affect him if he decides not to help. For example, he can now do his own laundry and get his own dinners if he doesn't show up and help participate with the family. Adra doesn't cook two nights a week, but has quick healthy dinners available so that she can get a jog in with her oldest child, or walk with girlfriends.

Adra has lost weight, started seeing a therapist, goes to a twelve-step group for spouses of alcoholics, and is now stopping the negative self-talk towards herself. When they are in public, Adra is more outgoing, and Alf is starting to look at her differently—as is everyone else.

Her husband has changed too. He now knows better than to comment on Adra's weight because, then, she just sleeps in the guest room, and he doesn't like sleeping alone. And, he doesn't like the feelings he has when he sits by himself with how he has acted. When Adra used to fight with Alf, he could just blame her for being a witch and give himself an excuse to drink. Now that she doesn't engage, he just has to sit there with his negative feelings!

Adra is feeling better, being kinder to herself and, by the way, Alf isn't looking so good to her anymore.

I wouldn't count Alf out yet. He may decide to go to AA or get help for his self-centered behavior. I have seen many couples change for the positive when one of the spouses makes healthy changes.

REMIND YOURSELF THAT YOU ALWAYS HAVE CHOICES.

No matter what situation you are in, you always have choices. The choices may not be perfect, but they are there. Don't ever forget that.

FORGET "FIXING" OTHER PEOPLE'S FEELINGS.

How people feel is how they feel. It isn't your job to smooth over uncomfortable feelings that other people have or to make people feel better. Your job is to be respectful, honest, and direct with people in kind ways, and to participate only in your part in relationships. It is okay if others struggle, feel bad, or go through difficulties. You can empathize and be kind, but no fixing! "Fixing" is detrimental caretaking, and it is bad for the both of you.

SET BOUNDARIES.

Boundaries are so foreign to Giveaway Girls that I've devoted a whole chapter of this book to discussing them. For now, suffice it to say that establishing boundaries is crucial to building and sustaining healthy relationships—even though setting boundaries means that people will sometimes get mad at you and you will sometimes feel guilty. The sooner you start practicing, the better.

REMEMBER, THE GOAL IS PROGRESS, NOT
PERFECTION.

All progress is back-looped. This is part of change. Any step
you take, no matter how small, is worthwhile. We're looking
for progress here, not perfection.

TRUST YOUR INSTINCTS

Nothing in this book is meant to shame or "tut-tut" your
decisions. Ultimately, you are the only person who can decide
whether a relationship is right for you. Just because someone
may not be measuring up now doesn't mean that they never
will.

People often ask me if they should "just leave" a relationship. Remember, we are all learning and growing, and we
usually learn the most from the people we are most connected
to. There are lots of tools and strategies you can employ to
improve your relationships, and change won't happen
overnight, so you don't have to abandon ship just because your
relationship needs work (unless, of course, your partner is
physically abusive, in which case you should absolutely
abandon ship, though how and when you do that is up to you).

So should you leave your relationship? Ultimately, my
answer to that question is this: if you don't know you need to
leave, then you probably aren't there yet. If nothing else,
there's more learning to be done. Focus on cleaning up your
side of the street and good things will happen.

OTHER RELATIONSHIPS

You can repurpose this information about intimate relationships for use in your relationships with other people. Many of
the dynamics are the same. For example, if you tend to have

difficulty asking for what you need from your partner, my guess is you might have difficulty doing this with friends, with your coworkers, or with your adult children.

Maybe you aren't currently partnered yet, or you don't want to be. You can use this information for dating, and use these tips with your other connections. You may now even have insight into why these connections have been such a struggle. That's okay. Start again. Now that you know better, you can do better.

Reflect on the equal-partnership questions and how they relate to your other relationships.

Are you a grandmother who is having difficulty with a daughter-in-law, or vice versa?

Do you have a friend who you find does all the taking and is causing you to feel resentful? (CDR doesn't happen only in intimate partnerships.)

Do you have a coworker who is inconsiderate?

Do you have an addict/alcohol abuser in your life who is causing you much stress and frustration?

You can use all of these strategies to address issues of concern or confusion in all of your relationships. With that said, let's move on to the workplace; there are a ton of opportunities to learn about yourself and what you may be giving away there.

CHAPTER FIVE

✧

GIVEAWAY GIRLS
IN CAREER

"The biggest human temptation is to settle for too little."
—THOMAS MERTON

As much as women detrimentally caretake at home, they do it at work, too. I have seen countless clients and friends struggle with detrimental caretaking in their careers; I have even struggled with it myself.

If you have any give-it-away tendencies yourself, I am confident that you, too, will recognize some parts of yourself in the stories I'm about to share—because if you're giving it away in any part of your life, you're probably giving it away to some degree in every part of your life.

The bad news is that detrimental caretaking is just as harmful to your well-being in your professional life as it is in your personal life. The good news, however, is that if you make efforts to focus on self-care and building self-confidence at work, it will translate into other parts of your life.

FEELING AND DEALING WITH THE PRESSURE

Looking more closely at all facets of where you might be detrimentally caretaking and deciding where and how your actions aren't lining up with how you want to be are the first steps toward achieving balance, freeing yourself from the self-imposed pressures you've been under, and helping you find more joy in your day-to-day.

This chapter will cover common Giveaway Girl on-the-job pitfalls, a breakdown of the four workplace weapons of mass detriment (WMDs) for women, and a primer on what to do about these issues. Pay close attention, Giveaway Girl: odds are, you've fallen into at least some of the detrimental caretaking traps we're about to cover. Here we go.

COMMON WORKPLACE PITFALLS

In Chapter 1, I introduced you to boundaries. Boundaries are limits that people place on themselves to protect and promote what they want and need in life. Boundaries are hard for many women because we have been socialized to consider others' needs before our own, so then when we start figuring out what we need, it somehow feels wrong and induces these weird "guilt" feelings.

The workplace presents several pitfalls for women caught up in the detrimental caretaking way of life. Let's take a look at what Giveaway Girls are going through. Can you relate?

OVERFUNCTIONING

Many women pride themselves on being the cogs that keep the machine rolling at their job. These are smart, hardworking women—women who go above and beyond every day as employees, women who can (and do) competently pull off doing three people's jobs at once. Problem is, they're giving way too much—and getting way too little in return.

When Joanne's company started closing things down and laying people off to save on costs, she took on extra responsibilities to help out. Her workload grew and grew, and before she knew it, she was doing her job plus several other people's jobs and barely even had ten minutes to eat lunch at her desk every day. Eventually—inevitably—Joanne burned out, overwhelmed by the insane amount of work her superiors expected her to do. When she finally quit, her company hired two people to fulfill the duties she'd been expected to take care of all on her own.

Why didn't Joanne's company hire a second person before she quit? Because Joanne was enabling the situation. She didn't have a firm grasp on what her own limitations were, so, instead of advocating for herself and asking for help, she just kept doing and going, hoping things would change on their own. But they didn't change—and eventually she couldn't handle the strain anymore.

Giveaway Girls can endure a lot. That can be a good thing in some situations—but if you never drop the ball, that means you're not giving anyone else a chance to pick it up. If you're overfunctioning at work because you've actively decided to take things to the next level there, that's one thing; however, women frequently engage in this hamster-wheel cycle even when there is no reward and/or it isn't necessary.

If your overfunctioning isn't helping you move up the ladder at work, or if you aren't getting paid what you are worth, something needs to change. Check in with yourself and figure out why you're doing so much: Is it because you actually have to? Or is it because you want to feel needed or have an exaggerated need for control? Is it because of a family role of being the "hero" or the "go-to" girl? Is this a good thing for you in the short term and the long term? Are you feeling afraid or fearful, letting the what-ifs in your mind take over?

If you're overextending yourself at work for the wrong reasons, start setting better limits for yourself. Instead of doing 300 percent, try doing just 100 percent. If you think you deserve a promotion or raise, ask for one. If they won't give you a pay raise, ask for vacation time. There's nothing wrong with working hard—but you shouldn't do it for nothing. Either use your overfunctioning in your job as leverage for better pay or a better position or for your own joy and self-fulfillment, or scale down, Giveaway Girl!

Always Saying Yes

Giveaway Girls are easy targets because they can be pleasers. At work, as at home, this often translates to their being taken advantage of. Competence and skill, combined with an unhealthy amount of yeses, will get twice as many files heaped onto your desk before the coffee has time to brew every day. Being exceptionally pleasant and accommodating might make you friends at work, but it won't help you with your workload.

My friend Sara—a single woman with no children—used to get asked to go to all the late-night functions for her work. Her partners (all of whom were married) always begged off from going, claiming that they had "family obligations." Sara didn't like attending all the evening and weekend events, but she went along with it for years—until she realized that it wasn't fair that she had to shoulder the entire burden, and her failure to speak up about it was just making it easier for no one else to step up. When she finally put up a fight about it, her partners agreed to start splitting the functions equally between them. Sara's much happier now—but she wishes she'd said something sooner.

Sometimes saying yes is a necessary part of the job. Saying yes all the time, however, is an invitation for others to abuse your willingness to please—and that kind of treatment eventually causes resentment to build.

Codependent depressive rage (CDR) isn't limited to personal relationships; it can happen in the workplace too, and when it does, it isn't pretty. Don't let things get to that point. Learn to say no once in a while—find a balance—and your day-to-day at work will improve dramatically.

Underestimating Your Worth

Here's a formula you need to be aware of:

COMPETENCE + LACK OF CONFIDENCE =
EXPLOITATION

I call this Formula E, and it's one that supervisors, companies, and organizations use all the time, especially with female employees. Some take advantage of it without knowing it; others knit it into the very fabric of their workplace. It goes like this: Take a chick who's supersmart, hardworking, and really good at what she does—and who has a proclivity for overachieving. Knock her self-esteem down a few pegs so she feels lucky to have her job at all. Add her desire to people-please to the mix, and what have you got? An employee who will churn out great work for lower pay, that's what.

Supervisors and employers who really excel at using this formula take it one step further by taking the credit for the good stuff these Giveaway Girls produce and blaming them whenever anything goes wrong, regardless of whether they had anything to do with it. And the Giveaway Girls themselves buy in without a second thought—or, at the very least, they keep their complaints to themselves.

Ever feel like you're the first to get handed extra work and thankless tasks? Are you still waiting for a raise after two years of doing the work of two people in your department? Has your supervisor ever treated you like a numbskull even though you know more about how things work than she does? You deserve better. Stop underestimating your worth—and stop letting yourself be a victim of Formula E.

Unfortunately, our uncertain economy and news of continued layoffs keep people on edge. You may not be in a position to set better boundaries at your company, but you can know your strengths, step up your professional development, make sure your contact lists are current, and start networking outside of your company. Opportunities are out there, so be ready.

Using Passive Body Language and Speech

As girls, we are taught to be "ladylike"—in other words, to use passive body language and speech. As women, however, we might come off as less confident and less competent than we are because of that passivity and behavioral style, which can hurt us in our careers.

Amy Cuddy, a lecturer at Harvard University, has done some very important research about how female body language usurps our power and decreases the respect others have for us. In a TED talk, Cuddy explained how important it is for women to exude confidence when they sit, speak, and stand. If you want to garner more respect, Cuddy says, you have to take up more space—literally.

As far as speech goes, I think all women should dump the "I'm sorry" thing. We apologize way too much, and we're way too quick to take responsibility when things go wrong. Sienna Miller's character has a perfect line about this in the movie *The Girl.* When Sienna's character is asked to act as if everything is all her fault, she says in reply "Everything's ruined, and it's all my fault? Sure, I'm a woman. I can do that standing on my head." Sound familiar?

Downplaying Your Accomplishments

Even extraordinarily successful women are guilty of downplaying their accomplishments. When Hillary Clinton was asked to take the secretary of state position, she gave a "Who, me?" response.[1] In an interview I once read, former secretary of state Condoleezza Rice downplayed her intelligence, saying that, sure, she was "above average, but not much more."[2] Regardless of your political affiliation, I think we can all agree that both Clinton and Rice are highly intelligent women who have accomplished a lot—yet look at how they have both devalued their achievements when put on the spot.

Successful, powerful women can be terrible at giving themselves credit for their own strengths.

There's no need to beat your chest to get attention from your boss—but you shouldn't pass off the credit to others when you're the one who deserves it. Instead of saying, "Oh, I couldn't have done it without John," say, "Thank you so much —I appreciate the opportunity." Draw attention to your excellent work—without being obnoxious or grandiose, of course. Healthy self-esteem is about owning your positives, accepting compliments, and not giving away your power to others.

DENYING DISCRIMINATION

The Shriver Report came out in 2014 with some disheartening statistics showing that women are still way behind men when it comes to pay.[3] Despite the fact that gender-based pay disparity is common knowledge, many women still have a tendency to believe that while everyone else may have this problem, they do not. This is a powerful psychological defense mechanism called "denial of personal discrimination," and one that women develop in order to make themselves feel better about their situation.[4]

Unfortunately, while this kind of denial may make you feel better temporarily, it's harmful to you in the long run. If you refuse to acknowledge what your financial value is and ask specifically, readily, and clearly for what you deserve, your situation will never improve. It isn't easy to advocate for yourself in this way—especially because the system is set up to resist your efforts.

As challenging as it can be to push for more, ultimately it's worth it!

THE FIVE WORKPLACE WMDS

Beyond the pitfalls we just discussed, there are certain weapons that bosses and coworkers use against women in the workplace—what I like to refer to as weapons of mass detriment, or WMDs—that keep women from standing their ground. These weapons play upon women's insecurities, and they're highly disrespectful. Many of my clients and friends have had to fight against such tactics at some point in their careers. The five biggest workplace WMDs out there are:

WMD #1

"You are too emotional."

How many times have you expressed a strong thought, feeling, or desire at work and had someone marginalize you with a condescending statement, look, or gesture indicating that you were being "too emotional" or even "hysterical"?

While writing this book, I saw a television political ad running in Arizona where a male candidate was running against a female opponent. Interspersed within the rhetoric, the TV flashed pictures of a screaming and crying little girl throughout the ad. It was a brilliant illustration of the "hysterical female" archetype that disempowers women. We know this as women and feel it often in the world.

This is total BS. Don't let anyone tell you that emotion is a sign of weakness. The truth is just the opposite: emotion equals strength. The entire premise of Daniel Goleman's excellent book *Emotional Intelligence,* in fact, is that emotional intelligence is a higher predictor of lifelong success than education or IQ.[5] Smart women and smart men know and accept this.

This is not to say that you should cry at a board meeting or shriek when your coworker disagrees with you, but it is fine to identify what you're feeling at any given moment and use it as a guide to help you do well in life—and you shouldn't let anyone tell you otherwise.

I have often told my clients that it is not okay for women to cry at work, as they are then perceived negatively. It reinforces outrageous stereotypes. This standard is completely ridiculous but true. So if you feel like you have so much anger, hurt, or tension that you are about to explode, go into the bathroom and pour the tears out there. Then wash your face and reemerge. It is just tension. And men who feel these things are doing themselves no favors by repressing the feelings or lashing out in rage.

For those of you who have let the dam burst? No. Big. Deal. It can be tough out there. Move on.

WMD #2

"You're wrong."

Women are prone to believing they are wrong—even when they are not. It's no surprise that this is true: we are subjected to constant challenges to our competency and major brainwashing that make it far easier for us to doubt ourselves than not.[6],[7]

Here, again, that passivity we discussed in the last section comes into play. How many times do men go around saying "I'm sorry" all day? Not many—but meanwhile, women do it everywhere, even in line at the coffee shop. This may seem like a small thing, but it exposes a much bigger problem: our unconscious complicity with a culture that questions our competency.

There's a pronounced difference between having good manners and being gracious and putting yourself in the wrong, or in the inferior position, time and again. The truth is, you are probably wrong in workplace situations far less often than you think or admit.

WMD #3

Boundary Shifting

If someone came into your backyard and started moving your fence around without your permission, you wouldn't stand for it—so why would you let anyone blatantly disregard your boundaries at work? But this is what Giveaway Girls do all the time: in their eagerness to please and get along, they let people push their boundaries so far back that they eventually cease to exist.

When I was growing up, I had to run and lock my door if I made either of my brothers really angry—I knew they could overpower me in no time when it came to a physical fight. If I could get the door shut before they stuck a foot in, I knew I had won. If they got even one foot anywhere near the doorstop, though, it was over: They'd push that door open inch by inch, and I'd have to face the wrath.

Your boundaries are like that door, and your coworkers are like my brothers—except they don't have to raise their fists to knock you around. If you know someone's trying to take advantage of your time, energy, and generosity, don't leave that door open; don't give that first inch.

Remember, boundaries are self-directed, and they belong to you. No one has a right to mess with them without your permission. You don't have to get aggressive about them, but you do need to stick to your plan.

WMD #4

Inappropriate Comments and Behaviors

Many women have a running inner dialogue that questions and counters their instinctive (and often healthier) reactions to uncomfortable situations. For example, if your boss were to say something inappropriate ("You're looking soooo good in that skirt"), instead of recognizing the clear boundary violation, you might feel embarrassed (*Is my skirt too tight? Do I look like a slut?*).

Why are you blaming yourself and not your boss for this boundary violation? Because you're a Giveaway Girl. Here's what you could say to yourself instead: *Wow. I wasn't comfortable with that statement. I feel uncomfortable and marginalized. I don't like my boss commenting on my body, especially when he has more power than I do. It feels like he violated my boundaries, and that's not okay.*

This doesn't mean you have to chew out your boss in front of everyone in the break room—although you would be well within your rights to do so! At the very least, however, building a healthy inner dialogue will help you to take a step back and consider appropriate actions and a sound response to situations in which you feel your boundaries have been violated.

WMD #5

Implicit Bias

My friend Caroline is a well respected lawyer in her field with twenty-five years experience working in law. Her boss Kate recently added a young male junior partner to her case. When my friend Caroline questioned her as to why she didn't allow Caroline to use her female colleague who had more experience, her boss replied with, "I just don't feel comfortable with two young women handling the case on your own." Well, that was very flattering and an example of implicit bias. It was flattering because my friend Caroline is forty-five and she thought for sure she was out of the "young woman" bracket. However, it was clearly an example of her boss being biased without any awareness.

Implicit bias is when people consciously reject negative stereotypes and consider themselves to be unbiased, but they unconsciously associate negative stereotypes in their mind. Caroline's boss had no idea she was being sexist and changed her decision when a male partner questioned her on the fact that she was discriminating and stereotyping. She was shocked at her own bias.

Many people, female and male, have implicit bias as a result of social conditioning.[8,9] Therefore, you will confront this wall over and over in your lifetime. That's the bad news. The good news is that you have insight and tools to deal with the copious practice you will unfortunately get!

POWER POINTERS TO TAKE TO THE OFFICE

There are clearly a lot of ways in which Giveaway Girls let themselves be pushed around or taken advantage of in the workplace. If you're allowing yourself to be a victim at work, it's time to put your foot down and start demanding better for yourself—whether that means higher pay, a promotion, or simply more respect. Here's how you can make that happen.

LEARN HOW TO SAY NO

Having confidence means seizing your rightful place in this world—and that includes telling people no when they push your boundaries. I know you were taught to please and appease, and that you probably think of "no" as a confrontational word. Perhaps you've even had a coworker who responds to every request she gets with an aggressive, intimidating "NO!" and you don't want to be like her. I get it.

Most of us don't want to be like those people (although I have to admit, I've always been a little jealous of their brazen willingness to be difficult and rude—it does work, that's for sure!). But saying no doesn't have to be so antagonistic.

There are countless ways to say no that are gracious and respectful. Creative, non-threatening ways to say no with a smile include:

- "Unfortunately, that doesn't work for me. Let's try another time."
- "I wish I could help, but I am *so* tied up."
- "I have a previous commitment/appointment I can't get out of."
- "I'm overcommitted right now."
- "Unfortunately, I'll have to pass."

- "My time's already spoken for." (No need to elaborate, especially if you've already marked that bubble bath on the calendar.)
- "I cannot do that right now."

Keep in mind that the way you say no is just as important as the words you use. Be kind but firm, and don't belabor the point. Once you've said no, move on to something else—quickly. Discuss a different project. Talk about your lunch plans. Compliment the person on what they're wearing. Do anything you like, as long as you don't give the other person an opportunity to turn your no into a yes.

Standing up for yourself and saying no with grace is about being seen and heard as the hardworking, diligent, caring employee you are. Your time is just as valuable as everyone else's! The recipient of your refusal may get mad, but usually that is because he or she is trying to shift a problem to be your problem, and you aren't allowing it.

Giveaway Girls are often afraid of people being mad at them, but that only enables the not-saying-no cycle. Don't fall into that trap.

DROP THE BALL A LITTLE

Sometimes you have to drop the ball to give others the opportunity to pick it up. I don't mean that you should look the other way when someone is having a heart attack—but if you're someone who thinks she has to be the one to do stuff or it won't get done (and if you're a Giveaway Girl, you probably are that someone), I challenge you to try out not doing everything. Chances are, you'll find that many of the things you thought no one else would do will get done. Take a step back, and you'll see that the problem isn't that no one else will step up—it's that you're just too quick to leap to the task.

Nobody likes an employee who never does anything extra, of course—but we all know that isn't you, Giveaway Girl. You're probably the opposite. So try taking it easy once in a while and giving somebody else a chance at bat. It will save you from getting burned out—and give others a chance to score.

LEARN TO NEGOTIATE

Women have to play by different rules than men in many aspects of business, including negotiations. Some people are quick to feel disempowered and threatened by women who come on too strong in asking for things. There is a definite gender backlash that can occur when women try to negotiate for raises. Others are completely comfortable with women demonstrating their power, and they even prefer a more assertive approach.[10]

It's important to know which type of person you're dealing with before you sit down at the table—but first you have to get to the table, which can be difficult for Giveaway Girls.

One of my clients, Kelly, was offered a job with a higher salary but turned it down. Her (male) mentor told her to use the offer as a negotiating tool at her current job to get a raise. My client felt guilty about leveraging the offer in that way; she felt as if she were doing something bad. Her mentor, however, insisted that she give it a try—and she ended up with a 30 percent pay increase. She's a single mother, so a raise like that made a huge difference in her life, and now, looking back on the negotiations, she's happy and proud that she made it happen. She built her confidence by trying and doing. But she never would have done it if she hadn't had someone knowledgeable on her side, pushing her to go for what she wanted and deserved.

If you need help learning how to negotiate, try to find your own mentor—someone who's good at playing that game and willing to teach you the ropes. If that doesn't work for you, and you find you still aren't able to ask for what you need, you may want to seek out professional help to find out more about what lies beneath this issue for you.

PUT YOUR NEEDS FIRST

From day one, Kathy's boss made her believe that all her hard work would pay off. "I promise this will be worth it for you," he told her. Meanwhile, he demanded 24-7 availability and commitment from her, meeting any attempt she made to set healthy limits with anger and hostility. She considered leaving more than once, but he always convinced her to stay ("What would we do without you?"). So Kathy put her life on hold: she didn't date; she didn't start a family; she gave her life to her job.

After ten years of promising that he would eventually make her the head of the company, Kathy's boss changed his mind, gave the job to someone else, and kicked Kathy to the curb. She was devastated. Here she was, approaching her forties with nothing (or what she felt was nothing) to show for it—no partner, no kids, no outside interests, and now no job. She had given too much for too little in return—a huge risk she hadn't even realized she was taking, because she'd trusted that she would get her reward at some point.

Ask yourself this: If the worst scenario you can think of came to pass, would the effort and energy you've been putting into your job be worth it? This is a good litmus test for whether you're pouring too much of yourself into your work. It's okay to sacrifice some things for your career—but if you're sacrificing everything, including your own needs, then it's time to check your priorities. After all, life isn't fair and sometimes bad things happen to good people. This question may help you set some limits for yourself, and with others.

BE CONFIDENT

Giveaway Girls tend to be competent but not internally confident. In the workplace, this lack of confidence can have an extremely damaging effect on how people perceive you—and, in turn, on your chances for success.

I hate that this is true, and it took me a long time to accept it. In my late teens and early twenties, I believed that competence was the key—that as long as you were really good at your job and had high standards for yourself, you would win in the end. Once I'd been in the workforce for a while, however, I learned that I was wrong.

Confidence is the real key; in order to be truly successful, you need good self-esteem more than anything else.

1.   CONFIDENCE + COMPETENCE = SUCCESS

2.   CONFIDENCE + INCOMPETENCE = SUCCESS

3.   INSECURITY + COMPETENCE = LESS OR NO SUCCESS

The first formula above represents the person who does good work and knows it. She demands proper treatment and compensation at work, and she almost always gets it.

The second formula represents the person who exudes confidence. She isn't really that competent, but she looks and acts the part—and she's skilled at getting others to do the real work for her. (When these people become supervisors, they attract Giveaway Girls like magnets.)

The third formula, sadly, might represent you, Giveaway Girl. You're excellent at what you do. You work hard. But you just don't have the confidence to back it up, so you don't get the promotions and perks that these other two people get. Instead, you get lower pay, longer hours, less recognition, fewer opportunities, and more burnout—all the things you never wanted.

The task here, then, is for you to act more confident. You can start by changing your mindset. Empower yourself with new ideas and tools, and then find people who will help support you as you implement them.

Do what feels right, and the rest will follow. And remember, you don't have to be confident to act confident. It's all about perception. It's okay to start out pretending more confidence than you actually feel; the feelings will follow later.

Gender shaping is partly to blame for our collective lack of confidence. Women have to be picking up on these messages all around us. In fact, I have met hugely successful women who quietly struggle with their confidence every day. It's totally normal, but it's something you can change.

Shout-Out to All Working Moms

If you are a career/working mother, you need all the help you can get. If you're married, ask your partner for help—either it's a partnership or it's not. If your partner won't step up and pull equal weight, lighten up on yourself and make more compromises. You can't do everything. If the extra help is expensive and your partner won't help, charge him for the outsourcing. I can think of few crueler ways to act in life than to leave you, as a mother struggling to care for your children by herself. Coping with parenting on your own without partner support can be traumatic and difficult. If you are a single mother, get help everywhere you can—and remember to treat yourself compassionately and with care and admiration. You have a lot on your plate; you're doing the best you can. Feeling overwhelmed anxious and depressed at times during this difficult journey would make total sense, especially given the lack of resources and support our country gives these brave and wonderful women. Self-care and Got It Girl strategies will empower you!

GIVEAWAY GIRLS AT WORK: PARTING THOUGHTS

All of us know what it's like to burn the candle at both ends to get a big project finished. And yes, going the extra mile when the chips are down is a great way to prove your loyalty and dedication to your job. But if you allow burning the candle at both ends to become your way of life, it will lead only to burnout—along with ashen feelings of resentment and bitterness.

Very few bosses, even the best ones, will tell you to spend less time on a project or to take more time for yourself. Furthermore, whether you maintain healthy boundaries or not, there will always be more work to do. So the motivation to work within healthy, sustainable limits must come from you.

Boundary maintenance is your responsibility. Saying no is a skill you must practice and cultivate—and so is knowing when to say yes. No one can do these things for you.

You may worry that taking better care of yourself will hurt your career, but the truth is, it's a win-win for everyone. The better your boundaries, the better you'll feel—and the more joy and enthusiasm you'll be able to give back to your job.

CHAPTER 6

⌒

WHAT SHAPES A GIRL'S ROLE IN THE WORLD

"Don't let the past steal your present."

—CHERRALEA MORGEN

I hope the idea that women are socialized to be caregivers, which fosters detrimental caretaking, is beyond dispute at this point. Women have long been expected to fulfill the "nurturer" role and still are today: various studies and surveys have found that caregiving professions in the United States are overwhelmingly female-dominated, and that women do almost all of the child care and elder care globally.[1],[2],[3]

Personally, I like being a caring and nurturing person. I am comfortable in that role, and it brings me great joy and life satisfaction. Is that because my parents—or society in general—taught me to be that way? Is it biological? A personality type? This "nature versus nurture" debate drives straight to the heart of the Giveaway Girl dilemma: are Giveaway Girls born, or are they made? Also, once you become a Giveaway Girl, can you change? In other words, can you unscramble a scrambled egg?

In this chapter, we'll examine the ways in which our environments affect us. Insight into why you do the things you do—and why you feel the way you feel—is an important tool for getting back the power you've been giving away. After all, the best way to get rid of a bad habit is to figure out why you have it in the first place.

FAMILY, FRIENDS, AND THE PUSH OF OUTSIDE FORCES

Outside forces are hard at work influencing your life. They have been there since you were little. It's time to descramble the coded messages you've received over the course of your life. Let's get started.

SYSTEMS THEORY AND FEMALE BEHAVIOR

As a social worker, I am trained in Bowen's systems theory, which centers on the idea that in any group or collection of people, changes in one person or entity will result in changes to the entire system. If a coworker slacks off, for example, others in the office may pick up the slack or intervene to correct the course. If a spouse starts to drink heavily, his wife may arrange an intervention, or she might rationalize and cover up for his destructive behavior.

A ripple effect happens because we are so strongly tied together with those around us. Culture, history, the belief systems of our social groups, our religious tenets, our families' values and prejudices, and even the neighborhoods we live in all color who we are and how we behave. Each of us plays a small role in a highly complex system that resembles, in its seamless harmony, a machine of interlocking parts. We all connect to the world around us—and in turn, the world connects to us.

The good news is, this interconnectedness means that the positive changes you make in your life can positively affect your universe. Taken in reverse, however, this means that the system you're born into has a powerful impact on shaping your attitudes, actions, and perceptions—and that's not always a good thing.

What's the world telling you? How many outside forces try to influence you on a daily basis? Are you even aware of it when it happens? The truth is, we can't possibly identify and filter out every influence that seeks to act on us; there are just too many of them. We can get better at recognizing it when others try, consciously or unconsciously, to take advantage of us, however.

We Giveaway Girls have to hold on to (or get back) our power consciously—or else we will give it away unconsciously.

THE PERSON-IN-ENVIRONMENT MODEL

Does your perception of your life line up with reality? To answer that crucial question, you must understand your world and how it influences you. A great place to start is the person-in-environment model. Here is a simplified view:

At the inner core, there's you. Your immediate and extended family members are closest around you, along with your ethnic heritage and cultural influences.

After that comes your participatory environment: religion, friends, community, and work. These are your peer groups and coworkers, religious/church affiliations, and even stores near you. Your social class factors in here, as do any voluntary agencies you support and the government and services where you live.

Beyond your inner circles, there are national, international, and cosmic environments—that's the rest of the world.

Around the other side of the systems are the forces of gender shaping, present and past traumas, and the range of life experiences you've had.

How do these various environments affect you, and what roles do you play in them? The ways you dress, act, vote, and behave on a daily basis may seem like conscious choices, and ideally they are—but all those people, organizations, affiliations, beliefs, elements, and more in those rings play a part in the choices you make. In everything we do, outside forces exert an influence—sometimes a profound one. Did you know that living in a certain zip code may determine your weight? [4] That is a simple but symbolic indication of the impact of your surroundings on you.

To better understand this concept, let's dive in deeper, starting by examining your individual system.

DIFFERENT PERSPECTIVES, SIMILAR EXPERIENCES

A Freudian analyst might say that giving it away stems from issues of unresolved sexual repression. A Bowenian therapist might argue that family generations pass down the energy that causes it, and the women in that family re-experience that energy as repression and dependence.

Addiction specialists might tag giving it away as "codependency," an outgrowth of the addiction dynamic in a family or a relationship. In other words, there are many theories on how the Giveaway Girl comes to be, and the one you choose to believe depends upon the framework you use to explain the issues and challenges of others and inform your perspective.

Based on what I've seen in my practice, I've identified a number of traits most Giveaway Girls share:

- They became Giveaway Girls at least partially in reaction to the "stuff" they experienced in their early childhood.

137

STOP GIVING IT AWAY

- They may have a history of addiction in their family of origin or their extended family system.

- They have a powerful parental figure who is also a Giveaway Girl—or Guy. (Yes, there is such a thing.)

- They never had a mentor/parent/role model who demonstrated positive boundary decisions for them to mirror.

- They may have been victims of physical abuse, sexual abuse, or neglect, or they may have suffered from verbal abuse and lack of consistent, emotional support/attachment in childhood.

- They assumed the role of "emotional caretaker" in the family as a coping tool.

- They are very responsible, nurturing, and sensitive people who are good at selflessly "giving" to others.

Giveaway Girls and Trauma

Trauma is defined as a deeply distressing or disturbing experience. Not all Giveaway Girls have suffered severe trauma in their lives, but many have. Why would a traumatic event make someone start giving it away? It's because when a person experiences trauma, a coping schema develops—and sometimes that schema involves becoming a pleaser, helper, or accommodator who subverts one's own needs, feelings, and desires and puts an "other" first.

Traumatization doesn't have to be an outwardly dramatic experience, like being held up at gunpoint or seeing something violent happen in war. A situation that doesn't look particularly serious from the outside can have a harrowing effect on one's well-being—it's all dependent on the person. For example, something as simple as having a mean teacher at a critical developmental stage can be traumatic for some people. It is not what happened but rather how it made you feel; essentially, if a situation has caused you deep pain, than you have probably been traumatized.

Trauma is a life changer: it affects how we act and how we view the world. Sometimes it can help turn us into Giveaway Girls.

EVERYONE HAS "STUFF"

Joyce Marter, LCPC, a renowned psychotherapist and owner of Urban Balance, LLC in Chicago, describes "stuff" this way: "We all have normal dependency needs growing up. And it is not possible for our parents, or their parents, or their parents to have fully met the normal, necessary psychological needs that we all have. So, we all experience some stress, anxiety, depression or relationship issues as part of the human condition. Hence, we each have our 'stuff.'"

Everybody has stuff. No one's exempt. This is partly because of "nature" (the way our bodies are wired) and partly because of "nurture" (the coping and self-soothing techniques we develop as a result of family relationships and stresses).

Some people are more open about their stuff than others, more than willing to admit that they suffer from depression or have an anxiety disorder. Others maintain tighter boundaries; they might know they struggle with anxiety and self-esteem in social situations, or that they have the same bad temper as their father, but—whether to protect their privacy, stave off workplace gossip, or present themselves in a more flattering light—they keep their stuff hidden. The fact that it's not obvious doesn't mean it's not there, though.

So where does all our baggage come from, anyway? For answers, let's start by looking at our birth families.

THE FAMILY LANDSCAPE

"Shh, little pitchers have big ears," my grandmother used to say when my mother or my aunts talked too openly about another family member in front of my cousins and me. I remember being confused about why she was referring to us as "little pitchers," but now I understand: children are like little, empty pitchers, just waiting to be filled up with their parents' feelings, values, viewpoints, and more.

Every family's members exhibit behaviors that are healthy, hurtful, adaptive, and, for some, addictive. Some families are healthier than others, of course—more balanced in the ways they connect with each other and with the world around them. Ultimately, though, everyone has at least some stuff, and whether that stuff is minor (like a behavioral quirk) or major (like sexual, physical, or emotional trauma), it spills over and pours into the next generation like runoff into an empty pitcher when it's not dealt with.

In my domestic violence work, some of the battered women I worked with told me how they had been brought up to think that they weren't worth anything—how they'd been treated as failures and disappointments from early on in childhood. I have witnessed the results of that kind of treatment in my own life: I grew up with a friend whose father constantly belittled and made fun of her older sister, Darla, in front of me and in front of other people.

"How could you not know how to do that math? What are you, stupid?" Darla's father often said to his daughter. He called her lazy and dumb and on a regular basis told her she would never amount to anything in life. When Darla hit adolescence, her grades plummeted and her behavior deteriorated—and her dad's verbal abuse escalated. He made fun of her fat body; he told her she would never amount to anything.

So you can probably guess how things turned out: Darla —despite her middle-class background—became a high school dropout, had several kids with several drug-addicted daddies, and ended up going to jail for stealing. I ran into my old friend several years ago. He and his dad couldn't believe how badly Darla had "turned out." "Can you believe it?" my friend asked me.

Yes, I can. And while I lost track of Darla long ago, I hope she figured out a different path for herself.

Not all parents influence their children in such an obvious and negative way. Moreover, most of what parents teach their children is worthwhile, useful, and done in a loving way for purposes of teaching and guiding. Most are doing their best and doing much good! Yet, some parents talk the right talk but don't walk the right walk. And I get it. It is hard to teach our kids by example.

At their introductory sessions, many of my clients go to great pains to emphasize how great their childhood was, how their parents always acted in loving ways and expressed healthy ideas of how they should live in the world. I believe them. As a result, they learned many great and valuable things from the people who love them the most. Yet, even those people who love and care for us can sometimes unknowingly teach us some not-so-great things. Consequently, even people who had a "really great childhood" can pick up bad or unhealthy habits from their parents without even realizing it.

Many mothers tell their daughters to act assertive, to be nobody's doormat, and to have a healthy life—but they weren't able to do that themselves, despite good intentions. The unhealthy sacrificing and people-pleasing these moms engaged in taught their kids (sons and daughters) to do the same—and their behavior has far more impact than their advice. "The walk" trumps "the talk" every time.

I believe it is insensitive, inaccurate, and unnecessary to skewer mothers who were unable to role model a balanced life and quality self-care for their children. (Remember the mother "blame thing" I wrote about in Chapter 3?) After all, these parents were just doing the best they could with what women and mothers were taught to do. In addition, most did well with all the knowledge, experience, and options they had. However, this "giveawayism" still got passed along, unintentionally, to some Giveaway Girls.

I love the scene in the movie *The Joy Luck Club* between a mother and a daughter that exemplifies this dynamic. One of the mothers is confronting her daughter on not valuing herself with her husband. This mother exclaimed this to her:

> "This not knowing your worth ... and even though I taught my daughter this, still she came out the same way [as me]. Maybe it is because she was born to me and she was born a girl and I was born to my mother and I was born a girl ... All of us like stairs, one step after another. Going up and going down but always going the same way. But now this cannot be—this not knowing what you are worth!"

Well said!

Still, the family landscape determines the predominant conditions of your upbringing, and a few landscapes in particular that fall within this category seem to produce Giveaway Girls in overwhelming amounts: the addiction landscape, the codependency landscape, the martyr landscape, and the abuse/neglect landscape. We'll take a closer look at them here.

THE ADDICTION LANDSCAPE

Families with addictions breed Giveaway Girls and Giveaway Guys with amazing proficiency—and yet many people who grew up in an addiction landscape don't even recognize it as such.

When I ask a client, "Are either of your parents an alcoholic?" I almost always get a shocked and embarrassed "no!" in response. But if I ask about a specific parent and certain behaviors—"How many drinks did your mom typically have each day? Do you remember your father taking any prescription pills when you were a kid?"—I usually get a very different reply. The person who wouldn't dare label Mom an alcoholic might still answer with ease, "Mom always had five martinis a day, starting at noon, and fell asleep on the couch before she could put us kids to bed."

Kids are highly adaptable, and they can learn to grow up in an addictive landscape as though it were normal—but there's nothing remotely normal, or stable, about it. Living with an addict is like living in a combat zone, always waiting for the next bomb to go off. It falls to the more stable family members to "clean up the mess" the addict makes—a cycle that is often the genesis for more extreme Giveaway Girl tendencies. Addiction also leads to feelings of what therapists call "learned helplessness" (more on that later in this chapter) in those affected by it, because they have little hope for influencing or experiencing positive change, which can also promote Giveaway Girl behaviors.

THE CODEPENDENCY LANDSCAPE

"Codependence" became a much more prevalent term in the 1980s, after Melody Beattie wrote her breakthrough book *Codependent No More.*[5] (You have to read her books, Giveaway Girl!) Codependents, as Beattie explains in her book, are women and men who are committed to imbalanced and unhealthy relationships (often, though not always, with addicts). Codependents focus on others' problems and addictions instead of their own, to their detriment.

Giveaway Girls who grow up in a codependent landscape are practically hardwired for detrimental caretaking; it's what they're used to, after all.

In the beginning of the book, we talked about how these codependent behaviors are unhealthy and an easy way to have an unhappy life. By now, we have learned how these things have been taught to us as a way to live. I know, I know—what a setup.

THE MARTYR LANDSCAPE

Some Giveaway Girls are affected by having seen a parent who played the martyr role. Perhaps they had a mother who complained steadily and felt victimized in her life. Maybe they had a parent or other role model who engaged in detrimental caretaking over and over again, but the parent never took proactive steps to change this for herself. Perhaps the Giveaway Girl grew up witnessing the overcommit–exhaust yourself–get no respect–worry too much about others–do it again cycle.

This Giveaway Girl may have heard her mother/father say, "Why don't I ever get any appreciation for all I do?" and then let out a few big sighs. Majorly guilt inducing! Growing up seeing and listening to this victimization modeling can help create a Giveaway Girl pattern as an adult. We will talk more about this in Chapter 10.

THE ABUSE/NEGLECT LANDSCAPE

When children aren't given the nurturing, connection, guidance, and care they need, it creates a sad and hurt space within their soul. In response, we humans tend to try to keep these bad feelings away from our conscious awareness. This is a natural inclination. We want to feel good, not bad.

When children are abused by a caregiver or even experience abuse at the hands of others (bullying, for example), their ability to know how to care for themselves is compromised. Sexual abuse is a trauma that indeed has terrible reverberations within a person's soul and could contribute to this unhealthy, detrimental caretaking dynamic. In addition, childhood neglect of any kind (emotional, physical, financial, or medical) can complicate people's ability to care well for themselves. Therefore, abuse and/or neglect paves the way for coping mechanisms like detrimental caretaking. Caring for others can feel like putting a Band-Aid on this painful stuff; the constant going, doing, and fixing for others can serve as a whopping distraction from those bad feelings we humans tend to resist.

Sadly, even small doses of neglect or hurt when one is young can make powerful imprints that allow "giving it away" to take place. Knowing this and dealing with those painful parts has to happen sometime. Better that it starts (or continues) now, with a new, more self-loving and compassionate frame of mind.

QUESTIONS TO ASK YOURSELF

What did your parents and the other adults around you show you, through their behavior, about leading a healthy, balanced lifestyle? I know and believe that they probably did the best they could with what they knew.

Did your parents share their joys and concerns in an open, honest fashion? Did they show mutual respect both in words and deeds? What about you? Did you grow up with a feeling of physical and emotional safety? Did you grow up able to use your voice in and outside your home to effect change? What did your parents teach you about what you could be and do in the world? What did other people tell you or teach you?

Our early lives impact us deeply in terms of how we view ourselves and our place in this world. Take time to explore each of these questions, examining the positive and negative ways in which your upbringing has affected your actions and feelings over the years.

MODELING AND EXPECTATIONS

From the cradle to the grave, people and systems try to tell us who we are and how we should act. Even as babies, we're told where we rank compared with others: "John is in the 40th percentile, but he should be here. How many words does he know now? He should know two hundred; that's the average for his age."

And so we are highly influenced from early on, most of all by our parents. Much of this comes by way of modeling; in other words, we watch our parents do certain things day in and day out, and what we observe influences us in profound and often unconscious ways. The rest comes by way of expectations, especially expectations based on gender (which the World Health Organization defines as "the socially constructed roles, behaviors, activities, and attributes that a given society considers appropriate for men and women"). What society defines—and what our parents define—as "appropriate" has an enormous impact on our views of who we are and who we can/should become.

Multiple studies have shown that self-confidence drops dramatically for girls as they begin entering their teen years.[6] Many girls start out feeling competent and confident but start to lose those feelings of power as they begin to change into women. A huge national report sponsored by Dove asserts that seven out of ten girls report that they don't believe they are good enough and don't measure up.[7] And depression is more prevalent among girls than among boys.[8]

I will add that as girls grow into women, they are taught to forget who they are and adopt accepted gender roles—and too often, those roles are defined by people's willingness to "give it away," again and again. Some girls see this and are able to resist, while others are not. With that in mind, Giveaway Girl, ask yourself: What actions and pursuits was I taught were acceptable and unacceptable? Whom did I accept and embrace as my role models as a girl, and how have those role models influenced me?

CULTURAL EXPECTATIONS

Some cultures are much more likely to expect women to be subservient and self-sacrificing. Going into this idea in depth is impossible, because it would fill another book (and that's a DEF-score no!).

If you are a minority woman, you already know and sense what the expectations are for you in your culture. You have been dealing with these messages and the confusing feelings they cause within you all your life. I have spoken to women who are Polish, and they describe serious expectations for demurring and deferring to men. I worked with an intern who headed up a Hispanic teen pregnancy program and she said the girls spoke often about the machismo culture and how the girls feel hard pressed to care for and sacrifice for the males in their lives.

In the movie *My Big Fat Greek Wedding*, the main character hilariously tries to differentiate herself from the expectation of self-sacrifice within her Greek community. In addition, African American women in our society have enormous pressures and carry the stigma of African American female stereotypes within our culture. They report struggling on many levels with issues of self-care, giving, self-reliance, discrimination, confusion about finding a worthy partner, etc. Handling all of these issue within the context of intense discrimination has to be incredibly difficult and challenging. However, all of these women I have mentioned are incredible and up to the tasks at hand! They have all already come so far.

For the Caucasian female, who has benefited from being a minority within the majority class: if you think you have it hard, think about the women who are discriminated against for their race or culture, on top of being female. *Wow!* These women have even more pushing and pulling against them.

The good news is that despite some enormous differences, ladies, we are all in this together.

TREATMENT, TRAINING, AND DISCRIMINATION

How is the world treating you? Training you? Many women (and men, too!) live as though they are small boats in a vast ocean, constantly struggling just to stay afloat and feeling powerless to battle the strong currents pushing them back and forth. This is what learned helplessness does: it makes you feel as if you have no control over your life. And women are particularly susceptible to learned helplessness, largely because we live in a culture that encourages it.

That's not to say that men are consciously invested in keeping women down. I would argue the contrary, in fact: most men recognize women's worth and embrace a worldview that values them (I have two wonderful sons, an awesome husband, and many family members, friends, clients, and colleagues who prove this to me every day). But the facts and statistics available about women's place in twenty-first-century society and its institutions paint a picture that doesn't reflect that mentality.

INSTITUTIONALIZED DISCRIMINATION
IN THE WORKPLACE

Here are a few things you might not know:

- Women still earn less than men with equal education and experience. The 2010 Gender Wage Gap Fact Sheet, issued by the Institute for Women's Policy

Research, shows that women earn eighty-one cents to a man's dollar. Minority women, especially Latinas and Native Americans, are also much more likely to hold the lowest-paying jobs and be single heads of households.[9]

- Even Ivy League–educated women make about 20 percent less than their male counterparts—the White House Project Report states that among Fortune 500 companies, women constitute only 3 percent of CEOs, 6 percent of top-paying positions, and 16 percent of corporate officers.[10]

- Even in female-dominated fields, such as teaching and social work, men usually get hired into higher-paying and more powerful positions.[11] And in pediatrics, a medical specialization associated with the care of children, female doctors earn only 78 percent of the typical male hourly wage.

- Mothers in the workplace have it even worse financially than their childless counterparts. A 2002 report called "Motherhood: The New Glass Ceiling"[12] cites two case studies where employers "refused to consider an employee for a promotion because she had a child and the employer believed she should stay at home to care for her family" and "refused to consider a mother of two for promotion based on the assumption that she would not be interested because the new job required extensive travel." In other words, these women were told (implicitly and/or overtly) that they should give up their careers—all because someone in a position of power thought it would be a better idea for them to give it away to their kids.

WHEN A WOMAN BECOMES A MAN

In the book *Freakonomics*,[13] authors Steven Levitt (one of the world's leading economists and a University of Chicago professor) and Stephen Dubner (a *New York Times* journalist) bring up a fascinating fact: with sex changes on the rise, researchers have more data on how this operation can alter perceptions of a person's intellect and abilities. To illustrate this point, they profile Ben Barres, a renowned Stanford neurobiologist who was born Barbara Barres and transitioned from female to male as an adult. Barres tells the story of how, after he gave a lecture, one of his colleagues who didn't know about his sex change remarked to a friend, "Ben's work is much better than his sister's." Just one example of how his colleagues' belief in his intellectual competency increased after his transition, Barres says.

POLITICS: ONE NATION, UNDERREPRESENTED

The United States is among the few industrialized democracies that have yet to elect a woman to serve as president or vice president. Ireland, England, Germany, and the Philippines have all had female leaders. In fact, at the end of 2010, women held the top leadership posts in seventeen nations, from Australia (Julia Gillard) to Slovakia (Iveta Radicova). We trail behind the United Kingdom, Japan, France, Italy, Germany, Canada, and Australia, as well as Afghanistan, Cuba, the United Arab Emirates, and Pakistan.[11]

Having had a few memorable women leaders in the United States over the last decade (Nancy Pelosi, Condoleezza Rice, Hillary Clinton, and Sarah Palin), we might assume things are getting better. Are they? When Clinton ran for president in 2008 and appeared to be losing, many Democratic leaders urged her to drop out of the race for the good of the Democratic Party—"Give it away, girl!"—and when she refused, it created an uproar. Why? Because our society expects women to bow out quietly for the "good" of others—to take care of someone or something else, even a political party. If a woman does become president within a decade of this book's publication, the United States will still be lagging behind must industrialized countries when it comes to females holding politically powerful positions.

GIVING IT AWAY AND GIVING IN TO FEAR

Women are taught almost from birth to be fearful and afraid of the world. And we're afraid for good reason: when it comes to women and violence, the facts hit hard. According to FBI statistics regarding crime in the United States:[14]

- A woman is raped every six minutes.
- Every hour, sixteen women confront rapists.
- One in four women will be battered in her lifetime.
- More than one million women seek medical assistance each year as the result of domestic violence.

One of my clients once told me that her husband got up at 4:00 a.m. every day and jogged for an hour in the dark before returning home to prepare for his day.

"You should try it," he told her one morning, invigorated by his run.

"What, go jogging by myself in the dark, with no one around?" she said. "Are you insane?"

He was shocked. "I never thought about it like that," he admitted. "I never realized women had to think like that."

"We think about it all the time," she explained. "So much so, we don't even realize we're thinking that way—it just comes naturally."

This story reminded me of the drama that surrounded the infamous "Central Park jogger" incident in 1989. Trisha Meili made headlines when she was raped and brutalized in an attack that remains controversial to this day (five youths were charged and convicted, but in 2002 a convicted rapist and murderer confessed to the crime, his admission backed up by DNA evidence). People were initially very upset and wanted justice for the victim—but when more of the facts came to light and Meili's identity came out, the tide turned and many people began to blame her for what happened. (What the hell was she thinking, jogging in the middle of the night?) Public backlashes like this reinforce a belief that Giveaway Girls live by: "Best to live in fear, because if we take a step (or a jog) out of the box, we'll get it—and we'll deserve it."

Fear leads to abdication. It makes sense: women feel vulnerable in a world that perpetuates violence against them, emotionally and physically, and that vulnerability leads to feelings of fear and dependence. Faced with these feelings, women usually respond in one of two ways: either they get tough and learn to deal with it, or they become more susceptible to systemic brainwashing.

I went to a salon and got a wax from a Russian aesthetician once. As I winced—it was a painful wax—she spoke a few words in Russian, and I asked her what they meant. "It's a common saying back home," she said. "It means, 'Hey, if you're

about to get raped, you might as well sit back and enjoy it.'"
She laughed. I felt horrified and certainly don't agree at all with
her statement. But upon reflection, I realized that she was only
voicing a message that many women have internalized: "Hey, if
you're about to get harmed, you might as well learn to a) take
the blame, b) enjoy it, or c) keep quiet." In other words, give it
away, girl. Give it all away . . . .

For many women, fear is an obstacle keeping them from
living life to its fullest. I'll talk about how to face and conquer
your fears in Chapter 10.

JUST SMILE AND NOD

Stanley Milgram—the Yale psychologist who conducted a
series of controversial experiments in which subjects
administered what they thought were deadly electric shocks to
shrieking "victims"—demonstrated that even in extreme cases,
people do not question authority. It's no surprise, then, that
when authority (in the form of institutions ranging from the
media to bosses who quietly reinforce the "glass ceiling" at
work) tells us that women deserve second-class treatment, we
simply nod and go along—even though we like to think we're
way beyond that type of thinking.

This submission to authority ties into "denial of personal
discrimination," a defense mechanism we discussed in Chapter
5 that causes people to deny the existence of discrimination
against them. This is a cognitive strategy that we use to protect
ourselves from realizing and seeing what's happening to us,
and by and large it helps women keep themselves content in a
system where they get less than they deserve—but it also keeps
us from getting more, both at work and at home.

A 2008 report by the National Science Foundation found that husbands create an extra seven hours a week of housework for wives, while wives save husbands from about an hour a week. Is this right or equitable? I don't think so—but I'm in the minority. According to the NSF report, only 30 percent of women say they think this is unfair. If that's not denial, I don't know what is.[15]

The denial of personal discrimination is a distant cousin to a psychological phenomenon called Stockholm Syndrome. Stockholm Syndrome happens when people are subjected to extremely difficult circumstances for an extended period of time. Even bad, abusing, and terrible treatment from others can become a weird kind of "normal" and can be seen as acceptable.

The syndrome got its name from a 1973 bank robbery incident in Stockholm, Sweden, where a bank robber and his accomplice held four hostages captive for six days. The "kindnesses" the two criminals, Jan-Erik Olsson and Clark Olofsson, showed the hostages overshadowed the fear and deprivation they underwent, to the point that the hostages had tremendous difficulty seeing themselves as victims when the standoff came to an end after six days. One of them even became close friends with Olofsson—a convicted criminal who had walked around the bank vault singing Roberta Flack's "Killing Me Softly" as his partner threatened to murder the hostages.

So, can you see how this bad situation brainwashed the victims into feelings of nurturing and caring towards the perpetrators? Although a case in extreme, this reaction shows how we as humans can psychologically adapt to what shouldn't be adapted to. Eventually, no matter how bad or unfair the circumstances, we can learn to see anything as acceptable. And when the circumstances aren't really awful—for instance, if you're just doing a lot more household chores than your husband, or your boss says no to a raise but compliments your work ethic—it's all too easy to just keep on giving it away.

RELIGION: THOU SHALT KEEP SWEET?

As a clinician, I am committed to the individuals' right to worship and express their faith according to their core convictions and cultural values. Whether you are Jewish or Christian, Protestant or Catholic, Buddhist or Muslim, atheist or agnostic, I respect the sacredness of your spiritual walk. Believe what you want; I honor that. Moreover, we talk more about how about spirituality and religion is an important part of your self-care in Chapter 9.

Generally speaking, religion can be a beautiful and integral part of an individual's life and community. Spiritual sustenance and religious values have done amazing things for people and the world in which we live. On the other hand, and perhaps only when humans start inserting their own particular interpretations, religious rules and ideas can sometimes be used against us. And this is so powerful! Religion has always been a double-edged sword, encouraging both the liberation and the oppression of women.

Jimmy Carter wrote a book in 2014 called *A Call To Action: Women, Religion, Violence, and Power.* He suggests a strong connection between scriptural teachings and misogyny. He asserts that religious leaders have for a long time twisted and distorted religious texts to make women inferior to men. This is certainly not new news.

Throughout history, religious tenets have been taken out of context or been exaggerated in ways that have compelled women to make sacrifices that endanger their personal welfare and boundaries. The United States specifically has a strong Judeo-Christian history that dates back to the Puritan settlers of the seventeenth century—and in Judeo-Christian society, the ideal woman has always been presented as caring, nurturing, penitent, and self-sacrificing.

For centuries, when Christian women diverged from this sacrificing, obedient model, they were punished by torture, imprisonment, and execution.[16] American society today is far more tolerant, of course—but it still places tremendous emphasis on women as caretakers and nurturers of others, even if it is to their great detriment or expense[17].

It's true that Christian faith is built on a role model of sacrifice: Jesus devoted his entire life to healing and saving others, and that was part of his divine nature, according to Christian teachings. But Jesus was also human, and he took time away when he needed it, including forty days and nights in the desert to separate himself from others and commune with God. He said no when he really needed a break. He set boundaries and even got upset and freaked out on people at times. He questioned authority and valued and respected women. And yet many religions, including Christianity, do not afford women this same freedom.

Everyone can agree that some people in the Christian faith have used scripture and other ideas about women and subservience to rationalize keeping women down. However, this is not the only place where religious ideas can be taken out of context to negatively pressure women. One need only look at what is going on in countries all over the world to see the damage that this twisting of religions can do to women and girls. Anytime your beliefs discourage you from taking care of yourself in a fundamentally basic way, you need to pay attention.

I have a good friend who was an obedient and devoted faithful follower of the Jewish faith. Let's call her Tamar. She grew up completely obedient to the conservative Jewish beliefs of her family. Her family placed enormous pressure on her to obey these laws and to follow what they interpreted to be the guidelines of a dutiful follower. Therefore, Tamar went to the university her family expected her to attend, she observed all of the religious "rules" she had been taught; she even married a man at 21 because she thought she was supposed to.

Despite doing all of this, Tamar found herself feeling isolated, depressed, and unhappy. She wanted something different for her life. She kept sacrificing her needs for her family and for what she thought were her religious beliefs. Then one day, she couldn't do it anymore. She walked out. She left her husband and started a new life in a different community where she could follow her own ideas of what her religion was. Tamar decided she wanted to follow her Jewish faith in a different way.

At first, this was unacceptable to her family and her friends. For a while, she was cut off from these people that had meant so much to her. They had expected and required her to sacrifice who she was and what she believed for their version of faith. She chose not to do this. She decided to stop giving it away.

Tamar was brave to choose a different course for her life. I can't imagine how difficult that must have been. Now she tells me she really felt like it saved her. To have self-sacrificed and submitted her life for everyone else's interpretation of what her God wanted was just not something she could do.

As I stated before, one particular religion is not the problem in any of this. The problem comes when other people interpret what religion is for you, and they use it to get you to engage in detrimental ways. Women have to be careful about what they are buying into.

Many other religions and/or religious leaders distort and use sacred texts to champion self-sacrifice for women. Take the phrase "keep sweet," a favorite saying used by Rulon Jeffs, a longtime leader of the Fundamentalist Church of Jesus Christ of Latter-Day Saints, a Mormon organization. Jeffs used the phrase as a mantra to encourage people to keep their thoughts and feelings to themselves and not rock the boat. Women in particular were encouraged to accept a man's wishes no matter what—including allowing and participating in polygamy. "Keep sweet," was the tagline. When Jeffs died at the age of ninety-two, he reportedly had anywhere between nineteen and seventy-five wives, some of whom he married when they were still minors. The parents of these child victims participated in this abuse in the name of their religion. Who knew keeping sweet could be so bitter? (Note: I am not saying that Jeffs is a representative of Mormon religious beliefs at all).

Sacrifice. Submerge. Submit. For the Giveaway Girl, that's a recipe for disaster. The bottom line is, any religion that denies women their value or their right to take care of themselves is dangerous—especially for Giveaway Girls, who are already prone to exaggerated sacrifice. But you can do better. Make sure someone isn't using the Good Book, or its version of it, to beat you down. You can be devoutly Christian, Jewish, Muslim, or anything else and still take care of yourself. No need to "keep sweet," ladies.

If you want to look more deeply into this sacrifice and religion issue, pick up *Slaying the Mermaid: Women and the*

Culture of Sacrifice, by Stephanie Golden, or *Women and Self-Sacrifice in the Christian Church: A Cultural History from the First to the Nineteenth Century,* by Ida Magli.

FROM 1920 TO 2015: HOW MUCH HAS CHANGED?

In 2010, Kathryn Bigelow became the first woman to win an Academy Award for Best Director. When asked what women in Hollywood must remember if they want to be successful, she replied, "As a woman, you have to be like a dog with a bone. Everybody is going to try and take the bone away from you. You have to be a dog." Ask yourself: Does a hungry dog Giveaway her bone?

In 1920, women won the right to vote in the United States —but the Equal Rights Amendment, written three years later, had yet to become part of the US Constitution. (A total of thirty-eight states must ratify it; only thirty-five have done so.) Clearly, though women in the United States have it better than those in many countries, we aren't "there" yet—and part of the reason for that is that we often forget where we stand. I'm shocked at the naiveté and innocence of women who don't realize how their gender has been defined over history, especially very recent history.

In college, I had two roommates who thought gender discrimination was a joke. When I pointed out that their involvement in sports in high school was made possible only by lawsuits that led to Title IX, which forced schools to provide equal money and investment for men's and women's sports, they were dumbfounded—they didn't even know what Title IX was. And this is not a unique scenario; I've seen this kind of naiveté time and time again.

The thing is, people don't like to change, and neither do systems. But where women are concerned, we need change to happen, because the deck is still stacked against us—at work, in politics, at home, everywhere. Ultimately, it's only by becoming aware of the influences that these systems have in your life that we'll gain the power to step back, take a good look at what's going on, and decide *Will I act?* or *Will I be acted upon?*

TELL YOUR OWN STORY

You have the ability to choose where you go and what you do with your life, and no one can take that away from you—not unless you let them.

You don't have to know that cigarettes cause cancer to quit smoking. Knowing the deadly consequences of smoking, however, can help motivate you to make that change. Likewise, knowing the dangers that accompany Giveaway Girl behavior—and, more important, recognizing the specific ways in which outside influences have encouraged you to give it away—may help motivate you to stop giving it away and start taking care of yourself.

Now that you understand some of the larger forces that impact female behavior, you're in a position to descramble the coded messages you've received over the course of your life—whether from a dysfunctional family or from an oppressive pulpit—and replace them with words of affirmation and self-realization.

In other words, now that you understand why you've been giving it all away, it's time to start getting it back.

CHAPTER 7

⌖

FROM GIVEAWAY GIRLS TO GOT IT GIRLS

"All great changes are preceded by chaos."
—DEEPAK CHOPRA

I have seen a lot of clients go from being Giveaway Girls to Got It Girls. However—and I'm sorry if this disappoints you—it won't happen overnight. I would love it if major, positive life changes worked like a drive-through; if we could just decide what we wanted, ask for it, pay, and drive away singing, life would be a whole lot easier. But we all know it doesn't work that way. Change is a slow and messy process.

The good news is, just by reading this book, you have begun to make enormous changes in the way you approach life. You will never again engage in detrimental caretaking without experiencing some lightbulb moments about your behavior. Even without actively trying to, you will start noticing things, and when you notice things, you will start making some adjustments. And if you do actively try to make a difference—if you put in some real, conscious effort—just think what could happen.

In order to move forward with that process, it's important that you start out armed with some tangible ideas about what it is to leave your Giveaway Girls behind and step into your role as a Got It Girl. To that end, in this chapter we'll explore what healthy decision-makers look like, what they do, and how they do it.

HOW GOT IT GIRLS APPROACH LIFE

On the surface, the differences between healthy decision-makers (Got It Girls) and detrimental caretakers (Giveaway Girls) may appear so small as to be nonexistent. Like Giveaway Girls, Got It Girls may also manage everything from iPhones to Evite invitations in such a way that you might mistake them for their Giveaway Girl sisters. The difference, however, is that Got It Girls have clearly delineated boundaries that keep them at peace with their decisions. Here are several characteristics of a Got It Girl:

- She often manages her life according to a system of four "Ds": do, delegate, delay, and dump. Notice how only one of those four categories ("do") requires that the Got It Girl sacrifice her time; the other three allow her to hand off certain responsibilities to others, put off doing things until they fit with her schedule, or, if they're not really important, wash her hands of them altogether.

- She is a loving, compassionate, warm soul who contributes to humanity, friends, and family through selfless acts of giving. She knows how important the way we treat others is. She feels good about her helping and giving to others. A lot of times, she doesn't even need credit for it; she just does it out of the kindness of her heart and soul. It feels so good.

- She knows that saying no does not have to lead to conflict, and that even if it does, the conflict isn't necessarily a bad thing, because conflict can be productive. A Got It Girl can keep her boundaries firmly in place without alienating others. For instance, she may employ gracious phrases that allow others to save face, such as, "I'm sorry, that won't work for me" or "I can't manage that—how about if we . . . "

- She puts herself first while still acting in a loving way toward others. A Got It Girl makes sure her needs take priority, knowing that she can take care of others only if she's first taken care of herself. She's loving and kind, but she's smart enough to know that dangerous things happen when she neglects her basic needs.

- She knows she can't save the world but tries to do what she can, when she can, and she makes careful decisions about what to do to make a real difference. When others come to a Got It Girl with their problems, she'll listen—often empathetically—but she knows not to dive into dangerous waters unless it's worth it, and she can discern between reasonable and unreasonable requests.

- She gives advice and suggestions only when asked for them, and she understands that people should be free to figure out what is right for them. A Got It Girl doesn't need to tell everyone what to do, because she knows that having an answer for everything is really about being controlling, not about helping others.

- She enlists others around her to carry their fair share of the load. Got It Girls make sure their partners pull their weight when it comes to doing housework and cleaning up after themselves. Instead of trying to take everything on themselves, they ask others to step in and help when they need it.

- She doesn't give in to threats, coercion, or manipulation. A Got It Girl knows when others are trying to manipulate her, and she doesn't allow outside pressures to change her mind about her decisions and what is best for her and her loved ones. She stays centered and emotionally detaches in a healthy way when pushed to act in a way that is detrimental to her own well-being.

- She surrounds herself with people who encourage, support, and guide her and offers them the same respect she demands for herself. Got It Girls know they can't go it alone. But just as they would resist those who would make unfair demands of them, Got It Girls also respect the boundaries of those they depend on to help them stay sane and centered.

- She has a great sense of humor. A Got It Girl possesses two essential skills: she can laugh at herself, and she can get other people to laugh with her, even when she's not giving them everything they ask for.

- She has a strong, resilient sense of self. A Got It Girl doesn't define herself by her job, possessions, influential friends, or other trappings; she defines herself by internals, not externals.

- She doesn't care what people think of her. A Got It Girl doesn't let herself get wrapped up in self-doubt or comparisons. She knows that not everybody is loved or liked by everybody in the world, and she knows that's okay.

- She doesn't have an anxious relationship with her strengths. A Got It Girl knows what her strengths are, embraces them, and accepts compliments with aplomb. She also expects herself to make mistakes sometimes and knows that making the occasional error doesn't diminish the value of her strengths. She is not afraid to apologize, but when she is finished accepting responsibility, she is compassionate with herself and moves on.

- She has great insight into her "stuff." A Got It Girl checks in with herself daily about what might be triggering her and what she can do about it that doesn't involve being controlling or dominating or painting herself as a victim.

- The only approval she needs is her own. A Got It Girl is guided and directed by an internal source that's rooted in both self-love and love and compassion for others.

- She's not rigid; she stays flexible within herself. She sticks to her guns when she knows it is important. However, a smart Got It Girl knows that she has to maintain some flexibility. She's receptive to the insight of others and sees the value they bring to the table in her decision making. Life is fluid, not always going on a straight line. She accepts this and allows herself to change her mind on occasion.

Whew, that's quite a list. And living up to any of these measuring sticks, let alone all of them, might sound like a tall order. But remember, as amazing as they may sound, Got It Girls are neither perfect decision-makers nor perfect people.

What really sets Got It Girls apart is that they would no more give it away on a repeated basis than you or I would treat our checking accounts as if they contained bottomless amounts of cash. As you make the transition from giving it away to getting it, you'll find that the characteristics listed above—lofty as they may seem—will develop naturally. Moreover, this list of Got It Girl characteristics can help you check in with yourself, Giveaway Girl, so that you can see where you might be aiming for on that Got It Girl trajectory.

TOOLS TO USE: DEF AND BAR

Did you know that the average person makes at least seventy conscious decisions in a day?[1] How can that be? After all, a Cornell University study asserts that when it comes to food alone, we make more than two hundred decisions a day.[2] Whew! It's safe to say we make a lot of decisions each day, and that creates the potential for a whole lot of stress.

Got It Girls know that the less they have to juggle, the lower their stress levels will be. With that in mind, keeping things simple is one of the best things you can do for yourself. Who doesn't want to make their daily life a little bit easier, right? But simplifying doesn't come naturally to most of us— which is why many Got It Girls utilize the DEF (Daily Ease of Functioning) scale.

If you cast your memory back to Chapter 3, you may remember learning about this handy little tool—but just in case you need it, here's a brush-up: The DEF scale runs from a score of 1 (supereasy) to 10 (superdifficult/complicated). In order to use the scale in your own life, simply make a list of all the decisions you're responsible for making and score them based on how much they complicate your life. And when I say "all" the decisions, I mean *all* the decisions—everything from figuring out what kind of car to buy to choosing what kind of sandwich to have for lunch. If you can get into the habit of incorporating the DEF scale into your daily life—and adjusting the choices you make to the scores you assign things (think cupcakes versus cake)—you'll find that life will suddenly get a whole lot easier.

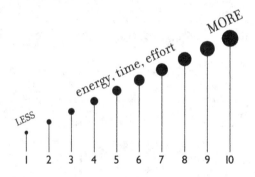

So, planning a party? Use the DEF scale when you're figuring out food, drinks, and decorations. Considering taking on a new project at work? Use the DEF scale to figure out how much you should put on your own plate and how much you should delegate to others. Dating a guy who's always messing up your schedule? Dump him. (Kidding! But do use the DEF scale to rate the level of complications he might bring into your life.) Above all, keep things simple.

When it comes down to it, what this whole book is really about is learning how to take care of yourself. Got It Girls have already mastered this skill. Giveaway Girls, however, still have some work to do. In order to help Giveaway Girls move in the right direction, I've come up with a simple, three-part technique called the BAR method.

With the BAR method, you ask yourself a series of questions relating to three important areas—balance, autonomy, and reality—and use the answers you come up with to design a course of action for yourself that reflects your best interests.

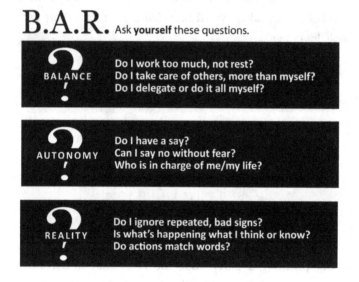

B.A.R. Ask **yourself** these questions.

BALANCE
Do I work too much, not rest?
Do I take care of others, more than myself?
Do I delegate or do it all myself?

AUTONOMY
Do I have a say?
Can I say no without fear?
Who is in charge of me/my life?

REALITY
Do I ignore repeated, bad signs?
Is what's happening what I think or know?
Do actions match words?

BALANCE

Have I found an equilibrium between work and rest? Between nurturing other people and practicing self-care? Between extending myself and enforcing my boundaries? Between meeting my responsibilities and delegating tasks to others?

AUTONOMY

Are others in charge of my life, or do I have the final say in how things go? Am I constantly in the role of the subordinate? Do I get to decide and decline without fear of retribution?

REALITY

Is what I think is going on actually happening, or am I deceiving myself? Do my actions and behaviors support my words? Do I say one thing (even if only to myself) and do something else entirely?

A Got It Girl in Action

In 2009, I went on a boat trip with a bunch of friends. One evening we were hurrying the boat in, late for a dinner reservation, when a group of people waved us down. Their motor had stopped working, and they were stranded in the lake.

"Rope us in!" they called out to us—very expectantly, I might add.

We stopped to see what we could do to help, of course, but it quickly became apparent that they were all wasted from drinking too much and weren't doing anything to help themselves. They hadn't even called for help, and now that we were there, they were sitting there, drinking their beers and expecting us to take care of everything for them.

When she realized what the situation was, my friend Ladonna—a Got It Girl if I ever met one—made an executive decision. "Come on, guys," she said. "Let's chuck them some beers and get the f@# out of here."*

As soon as she said it, the rest of us realized that she was right. We tossed a few beers to the other boat, went in and told the people at the docks that there was a boat on the water that needed to be towed in, and left —and we made it to our dinner reservation on time.

Ladonna may have her own unique style, but she's a happy—and not often overwhelmed—Got It Girl.

∘◈

A New Path for Living Well

So, we know what Got It Girls look like, and we've discussed some of the tools they use to take care of themselves even when they're taking care of others, too. Let's put it all together now and talk about what Got It Girls do on a daily basis to make their own lives better.

Got It Girls Ask for Help

Women come into my office all the time lamenting how no one is taking care of them in the way in which they are taking care of everyone else. What these Giveaway Girls fail to recognize—and what all Got It Girls know—is that you have to be helpable in order to receive support.

Going to a therapist is an important and courageous step in asking for help, enlisting support, and being helpable.

However, in order to explain a Giveaway Girl's role in this not-getting-enough-help dynamic, I often have to use my office plant as an example of how to be helpable. Bear with me here...

I used to have a plant in my office that was tough. I rarely watered it, but it survived anyway. Once in a blue moon, however, I would notice that the leaves were looking a little crispy and brown at the edges. Then, and only then—when it seemed like the plant was asking for it—would I think to dump a few cups of water in the pot. I recognized those withering leaves as a call for help, and I answered the call. As long as the plant seemed healthy and happy, though, I didn't think to give it anything.

People are not plants, obviously—but that makes it even sillier for us not to ask others for help. We don't have to wait until our leaves are droopy and brown to get the attention we need; we all have a voice that we can use anytime we like. But Giveaway Girls have trouble with this. They want others to see that they need support and help—they want to be watered —but they never look like they need it, and they don't like to ask for it, so no one thinks to offer it.

Got it Girls, on the other hand, have no trouble whatsoever with asking for help. They ask their boss for flexible hours. They call in sick when they need a mental health day. They ask their neighbor to pick up their kids at school when they are in a pinch. They ask their partner to meet them halfway. And when they receive the help they've requested, they really appreciate it—but they don't feel guilty about it, because they know that receiving support and care from others is part of what living a rich life is all about.

GOT IT GIRLS FIGURE OUT WHAT THEY NEED AND WANT—AND THEN THEY GO FOR IT

Got It Girls know what their needs are, and they trust their instincts. They understand that their feelings are a natural guidance system, and they check in with them often—and even when they are a little late in realizing what's going on with them emotionally, they make the right decision for them . . . no matter what.

Elizabeth, a fortysomething woman I know, is an awesome mom of four and seems to have a very loving partnership with her husband. He drives the kids around as often as she does. He coordinates playdates and cooks half the time. They smile and laugh a ton when they are together.

I asked Elizabeth once about their relationship, and she told me a story about how they were supposed to marry when she was twenty-three. They were just two weeks away from a gorgeous, huge wedding in her home city, she says, when her father came over one day and sat her down.

"Elizabeth," he said, "I just want you to know that the money I have spent on this wedding means nothing to me. If you for any reason decide that this decision is not right for you, I will support you 100 percent."

Elizabeth was stunned. She loved Paul, and she did think she wanted to spend her life with him—but her father's words made her realize that she might be getting married for the wrong reasons. It had seemed like the right thing to do—all of her friends were getting married, after all—but it wasn't really what she wanted. Not yet, anyway. She wanted a chance to live her life by herself before settling into married life. So, a week before the wedding, she called it off.

It wasn't easy for Elizabeth, of course. People were horrified. Paul was devastated. Even her closest friends thought she was making a mistake. Still, she knew what she wanted and needed, and she wasn't willing to sacrifice any of it, not even if everyone else thought she was crazy for making that choice. She stuck to her guns, found her own place, devoted herself to her career, and enjoyed her twenties as a single woman.

Ten years after canceling her wedding, Elizabeth realized that no one she'd dated since then had measured up to Paul, so she called him—and, luckily for her, he was still available. They started dating again, and eventually they married. She never would have imagined that things would end up that way, but she couldn't be happier with the results—all because she trusted her feelings and stood firm in her beliefs, even in the face of everyone else's judgment and doubt.

GOT IT GIRLS USE ALL EXPERIENCES, EVEN BAD ONES, AS OPPORTUNITIES TO LEARN AND TO EMPOWER THEMSELVES

Katelyn was attacked while jogging home one day. She fought back—and although her attacker did cut her hand with the knife he was holding (he was trying to cut her throat), she managed to call for help, and he was caught before he harmed her further. Rather than allowing the experience to make her feel small or weak, Katelyn says, it only strengthened her. After surviving such a traumatic event, she feels more empowered than ever before. She knows that even when things get tough, she can handle them.

Believe me, I know that not everyone is lucky enough to escape a bad situation with nothing worse than a cut hand; some people go through some truly terrible situations and traumas that have much unhappier endings. The point, though, is that Got It Girls are survivors.

No matter what life throws at her, a true Got It Girl can find a way to use it as an opportunity to learn and grow. Most of the time, this learning takes its own sweet time before you see it, but it will eventually show itself. Be patient.

GOT IT GIRLS USE GOOD BOUNDARIES

Got It Girls use their boundaries to help themselves. They know when to say when, and they are really good at setting (and enforcing) healthy limits. Sometimes they use boundaries directly, by saying yes or no; other times they get creative and erect boundaries without anyone's even being aware of it. Whatever their methods, they always maintain a good awareness of what they're willing to do—and what crosses the line.

I once worked with a woman who was a Dolly Doormat at work. Julie's bosses would expect her to do stuff like clean up dishes after board meetings and stay at the office while everyone else went to lunch; they never told her what they expected of her, and then they freaked out when she didn't complete a job that they'd never assigned to her in the first place. No matter how badly they treated her, she kept on trying to please them. Things weren't any better at home. There, she let her boyfriend walk all over her.

When Julie first came through my door, she was over-wrought. So we started slowly, setting small boundaries and working up to setting bigger ones. She focused on her office first—and after she'd spent several months of chipping away at the behaviors that had made her a walking target for mistreatment, things shifted. Julie no longer did the dishes in the conference room; they piled up into a huge stack for a while, but then, miraculously, they got done. She went out to lunch before the other people in her office had a chance to leave. She asked for a job list every morning so she could have a reference to point to when she was accused of not doing a task that wasn't hers to do. Once she felt good about what was happening at work, she started setting up boundaries in her relationship.

Ten years later, Julie has gone from Giveaway Girl to Got It Girl—one with excellent boundaries, a healthy relationship, and a fulfilling life.

GOT IT GIRLS PROTECT THEMSELVES FROM TOXIC PEOPLE

Giveaway Girls tend to take things personally and have difficulty unhitching from Toxics (difficult people who repeatedly make it virtually impossible to interact with them in a healthy way—in other words, people who drive you nuts!). Got It Girls, in contrast, have few interactions with Toxics. They make sure that they are not connected to them intimately, when possible—and if they don't have a choice about that, they keep their interactions with Toxics limited.

Essentially, Got It Girls minimize the opportunity Toxics have to do them harm: either they let them roll right on by, without giving the Toxics a backward glance, or they interact with Toxics when they have to, and then they move on without a second thought.

GOT IT GIRLS DETACH FROM THE NEGATIVITY OF OTHERS

I once had a wonderful mentor say to me, "It is none of your business what other people think of you." I love that so much, and I've come to realize that Got It Girls understand this, whether consciously or subconsciously. They spend very little time, if any, worrying about what other people think. They don't say to themselves, *I hope so-and-so wasn't upset when I told her I couldn't .... She looked annoyed.* When they do think about others' perceptions, they do so only to check in with themselves to make sure they did their best to be respectful and mindful—and then they let the outcome go.

GOT IT GIRLS TAKE HEALTHY RISKS IN THEIR LIVES

Ever watch the show *The Good Wife*, starring Julianna Margulies? I believe the reason that show is so successful is that the main character, Alicia, is a Got It Girl. She's a powerful woman who holds herself with dignity, warmth, and grace. She takes risks every day in her work and does what she thinks is best for her and her family. Even when her husband gets in headline-grabbing trouble for his own bad behavior, she never uses his failures as an excuse to give up on her hopes and dreams. She goes for what she wants and does her best to lead a life she can be proud of. It's compelling to watch—and a great way to live.

GOT IT GIRLS LEAD FULFILLING LIVES

How does one define a fulfilling life? No two people are exactly alike, so a fulfilling life can take many different forms—there's no one standard of "perfection" here. Really, building a life that brings you peace and happiness is simply about figuring out what works well for you.

One of my favorite Got It Girls, Alexa, doesn't have tons of hobbies or interests; for her, one of the best ways to spend a day is just to have quiet time alone in her house, listening to music and reading books. Knowing this about herself, she developed a job where she can work from home and set her own hours. Now, she gets all the alone time she wants and feels more energized to spend time with her sisters, who live close by, and her handful of good friends on her off days. She'll never be someone who enjoys drinking martinis and going out for a night of dancing—yoga classes and coffee dates are more her idea of fun—but she's okay with that. She does what she likes, and she loves her life just as it is.

GOT IT GIRLS USE YESES TO FULFILL THEIR LIVES

Got It Girls aren't just about saying no. In fact, there are some Giveaway Girls out there who are so afraid to let people in or open up their boundaries that they are too restrictive about who or what they let in. To try to step on their boundaries is like trying to touch an electric fence. These women have usually come from families with addictions or are with a spouse that has an addiction. They are so self-protective that they "give it away" by restricting themselves too much. They don't compromise with their spouses or friends or coworkers and if you don't fit into their schedule, you are just out of luck. They set their boundaries with their partners or co-workers very strictly, and they nod their heads but just do what they are going to do anyway. It is their way or the highway, people!

Got It Girls will listen to others' viewpoints and sometimes change their minds. They just don't do it in an unhealthy others-only focus. Got It Girls will include others in their decision making and they will use their boundaries to embrace and open their environment, not just use boundaries as a way to control, restrict, and constrict their lives.

CHANGED LIVES

I introduced quite a few characters in the beginning of this book who were stuck giving it away. Some were engaging in detrimental caretaking as mothers or partners, allowing their relationships to take up way too much of their bandwidth.

Some were putting far too much into their jobs and getting nothing back. All of them were unhappy with the status quo. When they realized their behaviors were harming them, many did something about it.

Remember Kendall, the working mom whose husband golfed constantly and freaked out whenever she asked for help? Kendall finally realized that it wasn't okay for her to be doing all the work all the time. She backed off some of her commitments at her kids' school, and she started taking one day every month to pick up one of her kids early from school and spend extra time together. She realized that she was overcompensating with the guilt she'd been feeling about how much time she was spending at work, and that she needed to scale back on a lot of things.

Tired of how much she was taking on at home, Kendall also asked her husband to stop golfing and to lean into their relationship, and his relationship with their children, a little more. He didn't quit golfing altogether, but he did agree to stop going every weekend and admitted that he had not been pulling his weight. "He was pretty crabby for the first few months when he didn't get to golf on Saturdays," Kendall admits—but now, she says, "we've finally found our stride."

How about Emily, the stay-at-home mom who couldn't lean on her husband because he was too stressed? She finally realized that marriage shouldn't be so one-sided, and she began asking for what she needed. When her husband more or less refused to help her or do anything differently, Emily didn't leave him, but she did figure out that she had to do what she could do to take care of herself anyway. So she got a part-time job, and she used the money to do some things for herself. She started going out with friends once a week, and if there was a mess when she came home, she ignored it and let it sit for a while (instead of banging around angrily in an effort to "punish" her husband for his passive-aggressive actions, which was what she was tempted to do at first). It was hard for her not to be resentful, but her self-care made an enormous difference in how she felt about herself. In short, Emily found healthy ways to deal with an imperfect situation—and for her, that was enough. Even though she and her husband still weren't connecting, she felt better and was having more fun in her life.

Remember Linda and Boxcar Joe? After much counseling, Joe decided not to do anything different and Linda dumped him. She went on to marry someone else and live happily ever after. Because of what she had been through, she was in an even better position to enjoy the true partnership when it came along, and she was grateful.

Anne, the woman whose husband kept sleeping with prostitutes, finally realized that he wasn't going to change and divorced him. Today, she is well on her way to leading a lovely, enjoyable life as a single person. She has taken up some new hobbies, including photography—and she has discovered that a beautiful life alone is better than an unhappy one with someone who treats you badly. You should see her now!

And then there's me: I used to be a Giveaway Girl myself. (Big surprise, right?) I was raised in a Christian family, taught by my parents that giving and sacrificing for others was the first order of being a "good" person. I was brought up to be trusting of others and to avoid conflict. And I still believe that these things are important—but as an adult, I have learned that you have to balance those things with caring for yourself.

Before I learned this lesson, I got myself into loads of trouble. I had a habit of making decisions without putting myself into the equation, and that tendency got me into some bad—I mean *really effing bad*—relationships. Oh, the stories I could tell. And on top of that, I used to work like a dog at my job, trusting the wrong people and letting myself be manipulated by others. It took me a long time to learn that not all conflict should be avoided and that I didn't have to do everything by myself. Today, though, things have changed. (Thank goodness.) I now think of myself as a Got It Girl—and I'm committed to helping you get here, too.

~ A Note from Cherilynn ~

I agree that when you read some of these Got It Girl characteristics, they could appear to be overwhelming or too difficult for you to achieve right now. The purpose of describing Got It Girls is not for you to feel bad about yourself, or for you to think that you have to be perfect at Got It Girlism to have a good life.

We are all human, fraught with insecurities and issues, and we are all just doing the best we can. Use this Got It Girl descriptor as a guide and something to aim for. Please stop yourself from thinking that these perfect women exist and that you will never be there. That's just negative, powerless thinking (not your fault!). You won't be perfect—none of us are—but you can aim high for yourself.

~ ~ ~

By now, I hope, you're already thinking about how you can use some of the tools and examples we've gone over to move out of the realm of detrimental caretaking and into the realm of healthy decision making. It's difficult to make good decisions if we don't have good boundaries, however, so let's delve more deeply into how to effectively set boundaries—at home, at work, and everywhere in between.

CHAPTER 8

⤳

GOT IT GIRLS: BOUNDARIES

*"The more you have to gain,
the harder other people will push back."*
—CHERILYNN VELAND

One of the most important hurdles a Giveaway Girl must overcome is her inability to set healthy boundaries for herself. Whether at home or at work, failing to set boundaries paves the way for detrimental caretaking—which, as you know by now, is something to avoid at all costs.

In this chapter, we will address the following key questions:

- ⤳ What are boundaries?
- ⤳ Why are healthy boundaries so important?
- ⤳ How do you set healthy boundaries?
- ⤳ Where should you implement this boundary setting?

Once you have the answers to these questions, you'll have the framework you need to build healthy, effective boundaries in your own life.

WHAT ARE BOUNDARIES?

Even if you're already well versed in what boundaries are and just want help implementing them, please bear with me and read this overview. This is an important issue, and reading what I have to say here might bring forth new ideas and thoughts that strengthen what you already know.

Boundaries, in their essence, are a series of tools we use to establish limits, expectations, and responsibilities. They help us define who we are and what we want in the world; they help us establish what's okay in our life and what's not. Basically, they help us let the good stuff in and keep the bad stuff out.

Boundaries are everywhere, and they come in many forms: physical boundaries, rule boundaries, emotional boundaries, time boundaries, sexual boundaries, territorial boundaries . . . the list goes on. Some are tangible and easy to understand; others are intangible and difficult to define.

I think the best way to understand the necessity and usefulness of boundaries is to consider territorial boundaries. Just walk down your street, and you'll notice tons of boundaries: sidewalks, storefronts, curbs, fences—even your driveway creates a boundary, an unspoken indicator of where cars should go. Merely by existing, that narrow strip of concrete tells people who come to visit that they are expected not to veer off the pavement and park on your grass.

HOW BOUNDARIES SHAPE HOW WE'RE TREATED

Good boundaries in our society prevent chaos and ensure order—and the same applies for each us on an individual level. Drawing your personal boundary lines and implementing steps to make sure they are respected is essential to keeping yourself safe and happy. However, since personal boundaries are intangible, we have to be vigilant about figuring what our own boundaries are, teaching other people what they are, and reinforcing them when necessary.

When we enforce our boundaries, we teach people how to treat us. When we give it away, we're telling those around us that we are willing to flex, or even break, our personal boundaries in order to satisfy their wants and needs. This is very dangerous for Giveaway Girls. It's okay to be flexible, yes —but in the right directions, and for the right reasons. Bending over backward to accommodate everyone else will only make you feel resentful and used.

RESPECT YOURSELF AND OTHERS

When it comes down to it, setting boundaries and learning to take care of yourself is all about respect—both for yourself and for others. It's not useful to demand respect from someone but refuse to reciprocate. You can't become a happy, contented, healthy person if you're treating the people around you poorly. But the truth is, most Giveaway Girls understand the "respect for others" tenet quite well; it's the "respect for self" part that they get hung up on.

One of the most common questions people ask me when I talk to them about setting boundaries is "How do I do this without hurting anyone's feelings?" The bad news is, you can't —not always, anyway. No matter how nice a tone or careful a phrase you use to ask for what you need, there's always going to be someone who will take what you say as a personal affront. But if you make respect for others a foremost consideration when you are setting your boundaries, then even if some feelings get a little bruised along the way, you can still feel okay. If you've set your limits kindly and respectfully, you've done all you can.

It makes sense that a Giveaway Girl would be more concerned with being nice than with setting healthy boundaries—that tendency is what's making you give it away in the first place. But in the long run, it's actually far more disrespectful to others not to set good, healthy boundaries than it is to repress your feelings out of a desire to be "kind."

NASTY NANCY

Twenty-eight-year-old Nancy, who came to see me after "freaking out" in an airport bathroom, is a perfect example of someone who waited too long to set her boundaries. Here's what happened:

Nancy was stuck in an airport with her two children—her thirteen-month-old daughter, and her three-year-old son. They were all exhausted and had been on a plane for eight hours, only to find that the airport where they had landed was shut down because of an electrical outage and they couldn't get anything to eat there.

While they were waiting in line for the bathroom, Nancy's son, tired and hungry, began to throw a tantrum. As Nancy's little boy cried, another woman glared at him and said, "What a spoiled brat!"

Now, Nancy was generally a sweet, soft-spoken girl. But people had been violating her boundaries a lot lately. Her husband wasn't helping her with their new baby; her sisters and her mother took for granted that she would always do everything they asked; and, on top of everything else, she had just taken on teaching Sunday school. When this woman yelled at her son, the dam burst.

"What did you just say?" Nancy asked, her anger rising.

The woman got down low, pointed her finger in Nancy's son's face, and said, "You are nothing but a spoiled brat!"

And Nancy lost it.

"You are nasty!" she shouted at the woman. "You are a nasty, nasty woman! *Nasty!*"

As Nancy yelled, the other women in line—and it was a long line; the airport was packed with stranded passengers—fled as if the bathroom were on fire. The "nasty woman" took off as well. Meanwhile, Nancy stood there in her ponytail and yellow sundress, holding her thirteen-month-old and the hand of her three-year-old, shocked by her outburst. Finally, she turned to her children and said, "I'm sorry you had to see that, sweetie. I guess even adults make mistakes in how they act sometimes."

When she got home, she scheduled an appointment with me.

Nancy's rage may have been aimed at the woman in the bathroom that day, but really, it was aided and abetted by everyone else in her life—all the people she'd allowed to use her to the point of exhaustion. After her explosion, she felt guilty about the behavior she'd modeled for her son in yelling at the woman in the bathroom. She understood the importance of treating others with respect (no matter how "nasty" they're being), and she hated that she'd let her anger take over in the moment.

Unless Giveaway Girls engage in active, honest, and earnest attempts to maintain a healthy balance and set good boundaries, their pain and frustration will build up, just as Nancy's did. When that happens, it's far too easy for the pendulum to swing a little too far in the wrong direction—far enough to knock respect right out the window.

Ultimately, then, you aren't doing anybody any favors when you teach them it's okay to treat you poorly. You can't expect people to give you what you need unsolicited; you need to model for them how you want to be treated. Believe it or not, some people won't know how to respect your boundaries unless you show them!

CANDACE'S BIG MISTAKE

Candace's boyfriend went out all the time, often staying out all night. After months of this, Candace finally told him that she wasn't comfortable with his behavior—she wondered what he was doing when he didn't come home, and it made her feel bad.

Instead of hearing what Candace was saying, her boyfriend shrugged her off: "Candace, you are so needy," he told her. "Relax! What's wrong with my going out and having a good time once in a while? I'm only twenty-two; it's not like we're married! Is this the kind of wife you would be? Man!"

Maybe he's right, Candace thought. *Love is about trusting someone. He's his own person. He should have the right to go out as long as he wants. I don't want him to think I'm some needy mess. Gosh. I wish I weren't so insecure.* She told herself these things, and then she apologized to her boyfriend for trying to "control" him. Then she spent the whole day feeling depressed, without knowing why.

What's wrong with this picture? No, Candace does not have the right to tell another adult how to spend his time—but that's not what she was doing. She was simply recognizing that his actions were violating her boundaries and sharing how she felt about it. Where Candace went awry was when she backed down and allowed her boyfriend's comments to invalidate her feelings—when she decided that he was "right" and she was "wrong." That's what made her feel depressed: she gave it away, and in doing so, she allowed the detrimental cycle she and her boyfriend were in to continue.

Here's how the cycle looks in the long run:

She feels violated, is angry and upset

Instead of saying something, she BOTTLES UP HER FEELINGS and walks around feeling like she's carrying fifty pounds of FRUSTRATING EMOTIONS

He keeps doing the SAME THING

She freaks out— and comes off as CRAZY

This further validates his opinion that she's acting crazy

She feels bad and backs down AGAIN

And so on

and so on

and so on

STOP GIVING IT AWAY

Pay attention to what this cycle does to Candace. It makes her feel disempowered, used, and sad. It feeds and increases any feelings of worthlessness and low self-esteem she might have even before she engages in this cycle—and she will carry those feelings with her to work and into her other relationships. Candace's feelings will affect how she acts everywhere. Whether she realizes it or not, her failure to set good boundaries with her boyfriend is dangerous not only to the future of her relationship, but to her overall well-being.

So what can Candace do? She can work on setting better boundaries. For Candace's sake and yours, let's look at how to do this.

How Do You Set Healthy Boundaries?

There are a few steps to setting healthy boundaries—starting with learning to identify boundary violations, and ending with mastering the use of a set of tools that will help you respond to tricky situations that test your limits. Let's start at the beginning.

Recognizing Violated Boundaries

Many Giveaway Girls don't even know when their boundaries are being violated. So the first step to setting healthy boundaries is recognizing when and how this happens on a daily basis. Sounds simple, but the truth is, boundary violations are often camouflaged by all kinds of complicated dynamics—like, for example, the institutional and cultural pressure women are under to "keep sweet." That pressure—combined with your own interpersonal experiences, self-esteem, worldview, and more—can make all this frighteningly complex.

It's because of this myriad of influences in our lives that so much of what I do as a therapist is to help people recognize what they are experiencing. Together, my patients and I explore the complex dynamics behind how the way they think and feel about themselves, and others, has evolved. We examine the approaches that prove useful, and especially examine the approaches that are not.

You don't necessarily need an "outsider" (someone not personally involved in your life) like a therapist or self-advocacy coach to aid you in this process; you can make progress doing this on your own. However, it's important to remember that changing a behavior is difficult. Breaking free of your tendency to ignore it when your needs go unmet, when you feel hurt, or when your boundaries have been violated is as difficult as overcoming an addiction. You must make consistent effort over an extended period of time. If you need help staying on track, a daily journal can provide a good avenue to self-awareness. I know, big surprise—the therapist recommends a journal—but it really does help. Sitting, being honest with yourself about what's happening in your life, and then putting it down on paper (or on a screen) can help setting healthy boundaries become more automatic for you.

Even without journaling, you can practice recognizing when your boundaries are being violated; remember, if you feel mad, annoyed, or resentful, you've most likely allowed your boundaries to be trampled upon in some way. Of course, some Giveaway Girls are so conflict-averse that they don't even allow themselves to feel angry—instead, they just get depressed. So if you're frequently finding yourself feeling depressed, sad, or even guilty, then that's a great indication that your boundaries are being violated left and right, too.

GIVE YOURSELF PERMISSION TO FEEL HOW YOU FEEL

Have you ever heard the saying "Don't pee on me and tell me it's raining"? I have a better one for women: "Don't shit on my head and tell me I'm 'just being emotional.'" (Pssst . . . it's okay to get mad at something that shits on your head.)

Couples come into my office all the time because they're struggling with major communication issues. I find that many of those issues stem from a predilection a lot of us have to argue with emotions. The truth is, emotions aren't always logical—and they don't have to be! They are part of what we are.

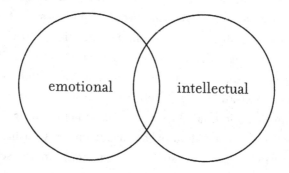

We all function within the two realms depicted in the Venn diagram above: the emotional realm and the intellectual realm. When couples argue, it is usually because one person is trying to convince the other that how the other feels is wrong. And guess what? That never works. Denying your emotions might keep things at bay temporarily, but eventually it will fail, because feelings are neither right nor wrong—they just are. How someone feels is how they feel, and you can't rationalize that away. Feelings function separately from the intellect, and they must be recognized, dealt with, and processed.

I can't tell you how many communication conflicts I've defused simply by explaining this simple fact to the person trying to rationalize their partner's feelings away. I point out to that person (and let's be clear: it's not always a man) that you can validate someone's emotions without endorsing them as rational. In other words, when you tell someone, "I see you're upset about such-and-such," you're not saying you agree with the reasoning behind it; you are merely saying that you recognize the person's feelings. And this simple act—just acknowledging someone else's feelings and giving them permission to feel them—takes the big red balloon in the room (the argument) and releases all the hot air from it. Ignoring that person's feelings, in contrast, will only make the balloon get bigger . . . and bigger . . . and bigger.

Many a divorced woman who finally leaves her marriage after twenty years will give you some version of the scenario I just described, albeit with different words and different examples. After spending two decades rationalizing their feelings away, not setting proper boundaries, not making requests, and not demanding to be heard, they burst. They explode into codependent depressive rage, get divorced, and have a midlife crisis. Meanwhile, their partner is left in a daze, saying, "What just happened?"

As a woman reclaiming your boundaries, you have to own your feelings. Don't rationalize yourself out of them; don't use your intellectual side to stuff down your emotional side. In the long run, you will only increase your depression, anxiety, and anger. The bottom line is, you feel how you feel. And if someone's behavior is making you feel lousy, that's your warning signal to stop and figure out whether your boundaries have been violated. Pay attention to it.

PMS, or "Permission Not to Mask Your Self"

~∾

Speaking of feelings, it's common for society (and men in particular) to discount what women feel during the premenstrual part of their cycle. A survey detailed in a 2005 Medical News Today article, in fact, found that 12 percent of men believe PMS is not real—that "it's all in a woman's head."[1]

To me, the raging of hormones is a gift. It allows frustration, disappointment, anxiety, anger, and depression—stuff that many women repress throughout the month—to push through to the surface. That angry, sad energy (yes, emotions have energy) must go somewhere.

To be sure, premenstrual dysphoric disorder does exist, and it causes misery in those women who have it. But a freaking-out, hormonal, upset PMS-er is sometimes just an unmasked Giveaway Girl who has failed to "feel and deal" with her emotions. So don't let the "keep sweet" ideology convince you to buy into viewing your emotions as connected to some sort of pathology—and feeling ashamed of them as a result. Instead, see PMS for what it could be: a wonderful way to access those (completely valid) emotions you've been repressing. Take note of what upsets you now, and address these issues later, when you are feeling better.

~∾

CLAIM AND RECLAIM YOUR BOUNDARIES: SEVEN TOOLS

TOOL #1
Respond, Don't React.

In the realm of human behavior, reaction equals a knee-jerk reflex. When you react, you don't think about your boundaries, assess your feelings, or weigh what you can or can't do to change the situation. This is where the term "reactive behavior" (as opposed to "proactive behavior" or "chosen/take-charge behavior") comes from. Reactions originate from feelings of powerlessness and rarely prove useful. Responses, in contrast, require you to think—and therefore empower you to choose what you do and say on your terms.

Remember: no matter how bad the situation, you always have choices. They may not necessarily be pleasant choices, but they are choices nonetheless.

TOOL #2
Make a Request.

Donna Panko, of Professional Skill Builders Incorporated, who teaches assertive communication and boundary-setting skills to Fortune 500 executives and employees, advises her clients that the simplest way to assert themselves is to make a request. She recommends using these words: "I would like to request that you . . ."

Sounds simple, right? Well, the formula itself is simple. In my experience, though, many women have trouble communicating these very words. They're afraid, in many instances, of how those around them will react. Notice that I used the word "react," instead of "respond." What does that say about the people who are intimidating these Giveaway Girls?

"I would like to request that you . . ." is a respectful, clear way to ask for your needs to be met. If someone decides not to honor your request, that's their decision. But rest assured that your stating things that way gives others the freedom to decide for themselves; it's not as if you are ordering them around or telling them what to do.

Hoshanna, a twenty-nine-year-old client of mine who worked as an executive assistant in a human resources department, was highly regarded by her boss and other executives because she was efficient, worked hard, and got along with everyone. However, she felt very frustrated that her boss constantly asked her to do things at the last minute. "Shoot, I have to leave to pick up my daughter at school right now. Could you please run the payroll and make sure Doug gets it before you leave? Thanks! You are the best!" her boss would say as she grabbed her coat and ran out the door.

That meant Hoshanna would spend two hours generating payroll, fixing a broken printer, and trying to find Doug's e-mail. Meanwhile, she was getting an entry-level assistant's salary while her boss was getting all the credit—not to mention leaving early half the time! This infuriated Hoshanna. She kept asking her boss to give her earlier notice, and her boss would say okay—only to violate the boundary again.

Faced with these constant boundary violations, Hoshanna decided to make some changes. She requested that her boss tell her by 2:00 p.m. if she needed anything else by the end of the day, and she let her boss know that unless she had that information, she might not be able to fulfill the boss's last-minute requests. Then, realizing that work wasn't the only area in her life where her boundaries were being violated, Hoshanna went further. She proposed that her husband cook on Wednesday nights and do the grocery shopping every other Saturday. She also asked her friends to keep their plans with her when she arranged her schedule to accommodate them.

After she made these requests, Hoshanna felt really good about taking better care of herself and communicating her needs in an honest, direct way to those who cared about her.

Maybe these examples can help you with situations you encounter on the job, at home, or in the potential disputes we all encounter:

- "I'd like to request that you talk to me in a different tone. That tone feels harsh, and it keeps coming up in our communication."
- "I'd like to request that you lower your voice. I can't concentrate on what you are saying when you are yelling."
- "I'd like to request that you consider crediting me, since you made several mistakes in taking my order."

Remember Candace? Maybe she could tell her boyfriend, "I'd like to request that you text me by midnight if you think you'll come home later than that. That way, I know you're safe and I can get some sleep." Depending on his response (or reaction), she'll know if he respects or dismisses her boundaries—important information indeed!

TOOL #3

Just Say No.

Ever wonder why this became the catchphrase of anti-drug campaigns? Just saying no represents a simplified way of using your voice to set a limit and cut off debate: no means no, and that's all there is. I have found that most Giveaway Girls have a hard time going from saying yes (to just about everything) to saying no (to even one thing). So, to bridge this divide, I recommend a statement that might feel a little more like using training wheels when you aren't sure you're ready to ride: "I'm sorry, I'm afraid that won't work for me. But let's try it another time." I'm not a huge fan of using the "sorry" thing—but, like I said, training wheels.

You get the drill. It's okay to say no! And you might find that if you say no more often, you will have the freedom to say yes to the things you really enjoy . . . and people will more readily enjoy you and the gifts you have to offer.

TOOL #4

Use the Broken-Record Technique.

Named for the way 45s and LP records would skip and play the same phrase over and over, the broken-record technique means saying the same thing again and again—without deviating from your message—until what you're saying is heard. This tactic is particularly useful for Giveaway Girls, because they can often be manipulated and confused by other people's challenges to their boundary setting.

Here's an example of how the broken-record technique might work:

Geri's best friend asks her to come over on Saturday night to help her scrapbook.

"Well, unfortunately, Katie, Saturday won't work for me."

"Why not? I thought you said you didn't have any plans for the weekend."

"I know. But Saturday won't work for me."

"Come on, it's really important to me. Remember when I helped you make twelve dozen cookies for that nightmare cookie exchange?"

"Yes. And I appreciate that *so* much. But, like I said, Saturday just won't work for me."

"*What?* You know I would do it for you. C'mon . . . we'll order pizza and have wine. It will be fun."

"I'm sorry. Saturday won't work. But, looking at my calendar, I can do it next Friday evening."

"Oh. Okay. I guess we could do it then."

"I would love to do it then! I'll bring the cabernet."

Meanwhile, Geri uses her Saturday to get things done, relax, and renew, and feels excited to scrapbook with her friend the next Friday night. It feels no longer like a chore, but like a fun way to use her creative abilities.

Here's another look at the broken-record technique in action:

Jane, a thirty-seven-year-old client of mine who worked for some finance guys in a small office in Chicago, was a consummate professional—efficient and competent. She knew before she started in her position that several former executive assistants there (all women) had had short tenures before they quit. Jane knew that was a red flag, but she had been unemployed for eight months at that point, and she needed the job. She thought she had to try her hardest to make it work until she could find something better.

It wasn't long before she figured out why all the other women before her had quit: her bosses were awful. No matter how well she managed their schedules, did what was expected of her, and pleased their clients, they consistently acted like she was an idiot.

Here's how a typical discussion went between Jane and her boss before she decided to set her boundaries using the broken-record technique.

"Where is the quarterly report, Jane? You told me you did it already."

"Well, I did. I thought you wanted it yesterday, so I—"

"What? I want it today. I don't understand why it is so hard for you to do these reports!"

"So 'hard'? What do you mean? I thought I did the reports the way you requested."

"Jane, why is it so hard for me to get what I need done around here? I ask for something, and then I have to come in here and ask you where you put stuff."

"Well, you told me to put it on your desk."

"Why must I do *everything* around here? It's not rocket science! Jeez."

Now, let's review this same situation with Jane using the broken-record technique to handle her frustrations and the criticisms her boss spews. Remember: Jane needs the job and has asked her boss not to treat her like this, but he keeps doing it anyway. So she figures out some standard phrases that she can use to respond neutrally, depending on the situation.

"Jane where is the quarterly report? You told me you did it already."

"The quarterly report is completed and waiting on your desk. Is there anything more you need right now, Mr. Brown?"

"What? I want it today. I don't understand why it's so hard for you to do these reports!"

"As I said, Mr. Brown, the report is ready and waiting on your desk. Is there anything more you need?"

"Jane, why is it so hard for me to get what I need done around here? I ask for something, and then I have to come in here and ask you where you put stuff."

"The report is ready and on your desk. If that's all you need, I hear the phone ringing—I'm going to go answer it."

As you can see, Jane's broken-record responses don't improve the way Mr. Brown treats her—but they do allow her to deal with his bad behavior without getting flustered, annoyed, and embarrassed for becoming upset and falling into his bad-mood trap. This technique frees up Jane to smile and feel empowered while she keeps her résumé ready for the next headhunter's call.

TOOL #5

Speak Your Voice.

Speaking your voice is so powerful—but for Giveaway Girls, it's also very difficult. It means that you "say what you need to say." What you say, how you express your feelings and give opinions, helps define who you are for others and for yourself —and being willing and able to speak your voice improves your self-esteem.

Just because you say something doesn't mean it will change anything outside you—but it will change you and how you feel in the world. If people react well to what you say and decide to make changes, great; if they react badly, consider it important information. People with good self-esteem surround themselves with people who support, validate, and encourage others. Constructive criticism, alternative ideas, and feedback are fine, of course—but they should always be communicated with respect.

Please remember that when you speak your voice and

make these shifts individually, you are helping our culture make these shifts as well. With every step you take, no matter how small, you are leaving a lasting legacy for our daughters and sons and for those that come after. Use this knowledge to empower you.

If your boss, friend, spouse, teacher, or parent doesn't support you speaking your voice, make a mental note. It speaks volumes about how interested they are in your well-being.

TOOL #6

Change Your Behavior.

Everyone knows that, ultimately, we have no control over anyone else. And yet how often do we actually behave as though this were true? Many frustrations we experience on a daily basis involve a desire to control others. When you think, *Why the heck is that guy slowing down when the light is green?* what you are really feeling is frustrated because you don't have control over what that guy is doing.

Changing your own behavior, instead of trying to control others, is great because it gives you control over that frustration. If someone yells at you, you can leave the room. If your mother-in-law calls you a bitch and says you need a nose job (yes, the mother-in-law of one of my clients actually told her this), you can opt not to spend any more time with her. If your boss insists that your performance isn't good enough no matter how hard you work, work less and spend your energy on updating your résumé.

My client Tanya and her boyfriend always fought when they talked about money. He would get crabby and act mean and condescending, disparaging her ability to figure out finances. Finally, she decided that whenever he did that, she was going to take a time-out from the discussion and use the energy from her frustration to help her fit in a good run. Eventually, she realized that since her boyfriend wasn't going to change, it would be best if they simply stopped sharing an account.

As Tanya demonstrated, you can set boundaries without saying a word if you want to, simply by changing your behavior—a great strategy for Giveaway Girls having trouble speaking up!

TOOL #7

Build Your Own Firewall.

Computers use firewalls to protect against virus attacks—to separate their stuff from someone else's malevolent intentions. You can use this same principle to protect yourself in encounters with out-of-control people. Let's say someone starts honking and screaming at you because you didn't turn right on a red light fast enough. You hear the driver yell, "You stupid bitch! What's your problem?" (I live in the city so the B-word is a common rant you hear from traffic ragers!)

Clearly, you're not the one with the problem. And if you have a strong boundary in place that will protect you when someone's issue, bad day, or judgment threatens your positive emotional state, as in the above example, you'll be much better off. This can be a behavior or a simple visualization—anything that will help you mentally define where someone else's boundary ends and your firewall begins will work.

Martha built a firewall for herself when she realized that her husband's bad mood at the end of the day was rubbing off on her. She initially tried to be empathic—to listen to his complaints, cook him a nice dinner, rub his back—but all he did was grunt and criticize, and after being home all day, taking care of three kids, Martha couldn't tolerate it. She tried telling him how she felt and asking him to stop acting so negative, but it didn't get better. So she started taking the kids out to the porch to play, or putting peanut butter sandwiches in a bag and taking them on a long walk. She realized that it wasn't useful to her (or their children) to be around her husband when he was like that, and since he wouldn't talk things out, she decided it was better to just leave the room and focus on good things until he got his post-work bad mood out of his system.

I have another client who uses the Wonder Woman stance—she crosses her arms just like beautiful Lynda Carter did in the 1970's TV series—whenever she feels as if her mood is being threatened by others' negativity. "No one knows what I'm doing," she says, "but it makes me feel strong, like I can deflect all those bad feelings away from me." She says it's really useful in her car. (I believe it—though I hope she doesn't do it while her car is in motion!)

Got It Girl Annie has told me that she pictures herself in a phone booth, protected by glass, when she feels emotionally attacked. It helps calm her down and allows her time to decide what her response should be.

All of these firewalls are about creating a boundary to help you emotionally detach in a healthy way from other people's negative stuff.

What is emotional detachment? Healthy emotional detachment can help us look at our situations realistically and objectively. Detachment is neither kind nor unkind. It does not imply judgment or condemnation of the person or situation from which we are detaching. It does not necessarily require physical separation: dissolving the relationship.[2]

I've shared these seven boundary tools because I think they represent the easiest-to-grasp, most effective strategies Giveaway Girls can use to win back their depleted selves. Give them a shot!

WATCH OUT FOR WMDS

I know we talked about weapons of mass detriment (WMDs) in the workplace in Chapter 5, but I'm going to review them a little here, because when you start identifying and enforcing your boundaries, you're going to meet with a lot of resistance, manipulation, and just plain ignorance—and some of that is going to present itself in the form of these WMDs. In order to protect your boundaries, you must be able to recognize it when this is happening. So here it is, a quick review:

WMD #1

"You are too emotional" or "You are crazy."

Remember Candace's boyfriend's response to her attempt to set boundaries? He told her she was being "needy"—i.e., too emotional. Don't let comments like these stop you from doing what you need to do in order to take care of yourself.

Emotional intelligence isn't a bad thing—in many cases, it's actually a huge advantage. Don't buy into the idea that your emotions are "bad" or "wrong." Feel your feelings, evaluate what's happening, and put a plan into action. Don't buy into the crazy-chick stereotype, either. Again, feeling and dealing with your emotions doesn't make you crazy. That's just bullshit.

WMD #2

"You're wrong."

People usually feel a strong psychological pull to keep things the way they've always been. If someone doesn't like your new boundaries, it doesn't mean you are wrong to set them.

Don't let someone else's resistance to change make you question your right to set boundaries you know are good for you.

WMD #3

Boundary shifting

No need for big explanations about why you need what you need—when somebody starts pushing against your boundaries, just know they are attempting to boundary-shift, and don't open the door for them to get in there. Detach and hold firm. Remember, you can assert yourself and still be kind!

WMD #4

Self-doubt and guilt

This is an easy pattern for Giveaway Girls to fall into, and probably the number-one reason they have difficulty setting and keeping boundaries. Tell your self-doubt and guilt that you see them, feel them, and know they are there; then tell them that you're making a good decision and they can't convince you otherwise.

Picture the unearned guilt as a childhood friend cajoling you into getting into trouble with them and tell it, "Thanks, but no thanks." Do this each and every time you feel the self-doubt and guilt that are so common when we first begin to set healthy, helpful boundaries. Those feelings will eventually dissipate, and the boundary setting will get a whole lot easier.

WMD #5

Watch for emotional manipulation (EM)

If you are trying to set boundaries with someone who makes you feel very confused about your boundaries, you are probably being manipulated. Some people are very good at this. As I have said before, Giveaway Girls are at high risk for emotional manipulation due to their trusting nature and reluctance to set good boundaries. Start paying attention to those that are trying to manipulate you. You aren't crazy! It's called EM.

WHERE SHOULD YOU IMPLEMENT THIS BOUNDARY SETTING?

Remember what I said earlier in this chapter about giving yourself permission to feel how you feel? This is the most important first step for you to take as you begin focusing on setting better boundaries in your life.

Spend a few weeks just paying attention to your resentments, hurt feelings, or other red-light indicators that you need some boundary setting in your life. Then start slow. I wouldn't go all gangbusters and try to implement all your boundaries in one day. Pick a small boundary and go from there.

As you go forward, keep in mind that it's totally normal to feel scared of or uncomfortable with this process. For most people, fear is a major impediment to implementing good boundaries. Just remember that if you're willing to tolerate some Giveaway Girl discomfort for a little bit, it will pass—and soon not only will you be okay, you'll be even better than you were before. The sooner you start, the sooner you'll get to the good part—so get going, Giveaway Girl!

CHAPTER 9

⌒

YOU: SELF-CARE FOR YOUR MIND, BODY, AND SPIRIT

"Plant your own garden and decorate your own soul, instead of waiting for someone to bring you flowers."
—VERONICA A. SHOFFSTALL

I t isn't your fault that you've been putting yourself on the back burner. We've established that now. Now that you know better, you must do better. So ask yourself:

- ⌒ What prevents you from taking good care of yourself?
- ⌒ What are the messages you tell yourself that prevent you from prioritizing your own care?
- ⌒ What are your family rules or scripts about this issue?
- ⌒ Did your parents model good self-care?
- ⌒ What have your beliefs about self-care and selfishness been in the past?
- ⌒ Have your beliefs changed after reading this book?

Answering these questions will get you thinking more deeply about this issue.

While reading this chapter, keep in mind the fact that I can't tell you exactly how you should be caring for yourself. You are a human being—too complicated, beautiful, and wondrous for anyone else to prescribe to you what must be done (or not done) to make you happy.

Everything you've learned here so far has helped to make it clearer what you can do differently on a daily basis to improve your experiences at work and at home. Plans are forming in your unconscious already, although you may not be aware of it. So let's step it up in this chapter and start creating a checklist in which you can begin deciding what you might want to incorporate into your new, Got It Girl life.

TAKING CARE OF YOU:
WHY IS IT SO IMPORTANT?

Taking care of yourself is important for two reasons: 1) because when you don't attend to your needs, you can never truly be at your best; and 2) failing to care for yourself can have serious health consequences.

Ignoring your self-care is like ignoring a flat tire on your bicycle: you go limping around, leaking air and under-performing. This kind of lifestyle leads to feeling half-full, half-happy, half-helpful, half-healthy, and half-there for your life and for everyone else who loves you. You have to prioritize your self-care and get the air just right in your tires to take on life 100 percent.

Taking care of yourself is about more than being at your best. One of the leading causes of death among women is heart attacks.[1] Why? Because women ignore symptoms and ignore their self-care.[2]

Most people know that stress leads to enormous health problems.[3] Well, ignoring your self-care will add stress to you and take years off your life.[4] You don't deserve that. Failing to take care of yourself can make you more susceptible to diseases and prevent you from having as good a life as you can.

You might think that prioritizing your own needs last isn't a big deal—but it can actually be a matter of life and death.

WHAT IS GOOD SELF-CARE?

Like many Giveaway Girls, you may hate the idea of taking care of yourself, either because it doesn't interest you or because you're too overwhelmed by everything else that's going on in your life even to think about focusing on your own needs—but that's too bad, Giveaway Girl. There's no negotiating on this one.

Taking care of yourself isn't just about getting manicures or maintaining an extreme (and sometimes even painful—bikini wax, anyone?) beauty regimen. It is about looking at all the parts of your life and taking care of yourself within that context.

Good-quality self-care is going to vary somewhat, depending on who you are. I suggest that you go through the categories, read about what a Got It Girl does to do well for herself in each area, and ask yourself what is missing from your self-care regimen (if you even have one). Make notes as you go so you don't forget!

BODY IMAGE

COMMON GIVEAWAY–ISMS

- ◦ Feeling bad about how you look.

- Thinking, *If only my .... were different, I'd be pretty.*
- Comparing yourself with others.
- Comparing yourself negatively to the "cultural ideal."
- Putting yourself down when you look in the mirror.
- Putting yourself down with others or friends, even if only as a joke.

A Got It Girl likes her body. She ignores cultural ideals and attempts to really love and appreciate what she has. She doesn't buy into the idea that you can never be too thin or too young.

I personally have a hard time with this one for sure—just ask my girlfriends. I have been trying to lose eight pounds for ten years. For some reason, I haven't been able to shake the crazy fantasy that I will one day be able to slip into my too-tight jeans with no difficulty, but I am working on that. I will eventually get to the point of accepting myself as I am. I have found that dressing in clothes that fit my shape nicely, doing my hair and makeup, and telling myself I look great does wonders—and at least I'm able to laugh at myself along the way.

DOING IT DIFFERENTLY

- Like your body for what it gives you. After all, it gives you the ability to be and act in this world. Embrace imperfection.

- If you really believe that you have to change something, make sure you're changing it for you and not for anyone else.

- "Joy is the best makeup," says writer Anne Lamott. So true. Want to change how you look for the better? Try finding joy in your life.

- Hate a part of your body? Envision an accident where it is destroyed. Wouldn't you miss it? I tried that with my saddlebags, and it worked. I felt really sad for the little guys, and I even missed them. It is a totally weird trick, but it works (most of the time, anyway).

Once, when I was twenty-one, I dressed up and did my hair and went out to meet a good friend on a beautiful summer night at a lovely outdoor bar overlooking a bay in Washington D.C. I was feeling very chic. It was dusk, and the mood was ebullient and sexy, the people around me sipping their drinks by the shore. I walked by a group of guys, and I saw one guy give me the up-and-down look that women in their twenties often get. I swooshed by him, and as I passed I heard him decry very loudly, "Cute face. Ugly butt!"

I was the only girl near them, and I thought for sure I must have misheard. So I turned around and walked by again to see if I was imagining things—and again I heard, "Cute face, ugly butt!" I turned around and made eye contact. I knew the guy was trying to demean me and make me feel like crap, but even though I knew that, it worked. I allowed it to work because my behind was something that I didn't like about myself.

Life can be like that: we're feeling good about how we look, and then—wham!—something happens to turn those good feelings into bad ones. I am older now, and my butt is bigger than it was when I was twenty-one, but I like it better than I did then (although I'm sure that guy wouldn't). I still wish I hadn't given that jerk the power to hurt me the way he did. We can't live up to others' ideals when it comes to our bodies—and we shouldn't have to try. That experience taught me a powerful lesson about self-care and giving other people the power to affect how I feel. We, not society, are the ones with the power to decide what beauty is for us. Don't buy into the hype.

Keep in mind, too, that anyone who watches what you eat, hints about your body imperfections, or even jokes about or teases you about things you are sensitive about—"friend" or stranger—is attempting to demean and control you. Cruel as his comments were, I am grateful that mean guy immediately told me what he was about, because it allowed me to immediately figure out that he was bad news. That kind of behavior will definitely interfere with your self-care, so when somebody does that to you, get the heck out of there.

PHYSICAL CARE

COMMON GIVEAWAY-ISMS

- Not exercising enough
- Not eating healthfully
- Drinking too much
- Not sleeping enough
- Overeating
- Undereating

DOING IT DIFFERENTLY

- Keep processed foods to a minimum.
- Eat healthy, balanced meals.
- Avoid too much caffeine and too many diet drinks.

- Avoid too much alcohol.
- Exercise at least three times a week for twenty minutes.
- Get eight hours of sleep each night.

I know a ton of women who are excellent at taking care of others, but when it comes to their own health and eating, they just don't pay attention. They eat on the run and don't make time to exercise, and the next thing you know, they're fifty pounds overweight and feel like crap about themselves—and yet they still manage to disconnect from their behavior enough to keep on doing it.

It is hard work to take care of yourself physically. It can often feel like a part-time job. Many people are so busy and running so hard that carving yet another couple of hours out of their day just doesn't feel worth it.

Maintaining a healthy lifestyle, a healthy diet, and physical fitness might seem like too much to handle. However, taking the time and making the effort to keep your body healthy is crucial to your overall well-being. Show yourself and the world that you care enough to make your health a priority.

MEDICAL HEALTH

COMMON GIVEAWAY–ISMS

- Ignoring symptoms
- Not resting when you are feeling poorly
- Not asking for help
- Not setting up and going to regular doctor and dentist appointments

I already told you that women are more likely to die from a heart attack than anything else—but did you know that women are six times more likely to die from a heart attack than from all forms of cancer combined? Or that one of the biggest reasons more women than men die this way is that they ignore their symptoms (self-sacrifice) and because they often get shooed out of the hospital without a diagnosis?

My grandmother Hilder died of a heart attack—by herself, in the back of a taxi—when she was in her seventies. Years later, I looked through her journal and she had written in there that she had gone to the doctor twice, complaining of chest pain, but he had ignored her symptoms and sent her home without any testing. That was in 1984.

Research shows that doctors are less likely to respond accurately to these issues, as well as when women report physical pain. Doctors tend to misdiagnose or under-respond to women. Be aware of this as you medically advocate for yourself.[5],[6],[7],[8]

Women don't pay attention to their symptoms and ignore their pain, even though when a relative or friend presents the same symptoms, women encourage them to get it looked at and seek treatment. I can think of no better example of the silent epidemic of self-sacrifice among women than this one.

DOING IT DIFFERENTLY

- Set up and go to doctor's appointments.
- Call in sick to work when you're sick.
- Call in a babysitter or ask your partner to help when you're sick at home with kids.
- Take vitamins.

- When you're feeling tired or run down, take a day off to rest and recuperate.
- Get massages or other supportive health treatments as a kind way to nurture your body.
- Tune in to your body and its needs.
- Do the things necessary to provide for and maintain your physical health.

I once went to my doctor in Chicago with a list of cold symptoms that I couldn't shake. I kept telling my physician that the medicine he'd prescribed me wasn't working. He told me to go home and rest, but I had a huge list of things to do and I didn't have time for that, so I ignored his advice and kept trying to convince him I needed antibiotics.

Finally, my doctor grabbed me by the shoulders and patiently and calmly repeated this to me: "You need to go home, lie down, and rest." Then he said it several more times.

I finally got it. I burst out laughing and told him I would do what he said. I went home, slept for several hours, and stayed in bed the next day—and the day after that, I popped up as refreshed and healed as anyone can be. It was a powerful learning moment about self-care—and I'm grateful to my doctor for imparting it!

Now, can you imagine going to the hospital with an injury and enjoying your stay? A girlfriend of mine once went to the ER after cutting her hand while putting away the dishes. The triage nurse there appraised her cut and called out to the other medical staff, "I got another mother here!" Apparently, moms were commonly coming in with cuts from putting away the dishes.

My friend was taken into a room, where she was given a blanket. The medical people asked her what she wanted to drink. Every few minutes, the nurse would peek in and check to see how my friend was doing while she waited for the doctor. My girlfriend relaxed in a quiet room. She read a magazine while she waited. She enjoyed herself. When the doctor finally came in, she told him what a nice time she had been having. She said the doctor looked up and told her that sounded really pathetic. It is, but most of us women can relate, and that is not good.

SEXUALITY

COMMON GIVEAWAY–ISMS

- Doing things you are uncomfortable with
- Having sex to feel desirable (not because you want to)
- Having sex or doing things sexually because of pressure or a desire to please
- Not connecting with your sensual self
- Feeling bad about or ashamed of your normal, sexual feelings
- Not asking for what you want and need sexually
- Accepting less-than-acceptable sexual behavior from a partner
- Not protecting yourself from disease
- Engaging in risky sexual behaviors
- Disallowing yourself to engage sexually in ways you desire

When I first proposed *Stop Giving It Away* to my friends and family, some people thought I was talking about sex. Sex is just one part of the Giveaway Girl issue. I have worked with women who have hurt themselves by having sex out of desperation and low self-esteem.

Theresa was a beautiful twenty-four-year-old who told me she slept with guys she met in bars. She said she did it because she felt so wanted and desired. She loved that feeling of being seduced. At the time of the seduction, the guys treated her well and seemed to care about her. Sadly, when she woke up the next day, the guys tended to drop all that seductive behavior, and she was left with feelings like shame, regret, and humiliation.

Severely neglected as a child, Theresa had addicts as parents, so she had been desperate all her life to feel desired, treasured, and adored. However, this casual sex was perpetuating the neglect and objectification she had felt throughout her childhood.

Through counseling, Theresa worked on making better choices about how she filled those needs.

DOING IT DIFFERENTLY

- ⌐ Engage in sexual behavior you desire or are curious about.

- ⌐ Don't engage in any pressured decisions.

- ⌐ Protect yourself from disease.

- ⌐ Ask your partner(s) to use a condom, regardless of their feelings about it.

- ⌐ Don't take risks that aren't part of your sexual desires.

- ⌐ Know that you are a sensual, normal human being and that your sexuality is a wonderful part of who you are.

- ⌐ Accept the sexual limits and choices of your partner while still feeling free to make your own decisions.

- ⌐ Ask for what you want and need sexually.

- ◦ If you have suffered a trauma that has affected you sexually, try to be loving and kind to yourself and address these issues with the support of a licensed mental health professional who specializes in trauma.
- ◦ Detach from the negative judgment and beliefs of others about your sexuality and your sexual choices.

I have met many Giveaway Girls who have experimented with the above common Giveaway–isms and found that they felt really bad about themselves in the aftermath. This is not to say that being sexually active is a bad thing; it can become bad for you, however, when you do it for the wrong reasons.

I have seen many Giveaway Girls engage in sexual relationships when what they really want is emotional intimacy. They use sex as a way to connect emotionally and then are devastated and hurt when it doesn't translate into something more meaningful. This is self-sabotage—the exact opposite of good self-care.

Conversely, there are women who are shut down sexually with what has been coined "sexual anorexia."[9] This is a process by which a woman's hurt, shame, or confusion about her attachments, her sexuality, and her relationships has closed down her willingness or ability to be sensual and sexual with those she loves. This is hard stuff, too, and can be just as damaging as the other extreme can be.

A caring, compassionate therapist can help you manage these issues, if you're willing to seek one out. It's something to think about; after all, we get only one life!

EMOTIONAL AND MENTAL HEALTH

COMMON GIVEAWAY–ISMS

- ☞ Not paying attention to your emotions
- ☞ Not knowing how you feel
- ☞ Not honoring your emotions in decision making
- ☞ Letting emotions completely dictate how you live your life
- ☞ Discounting or invalidating your feelings
- ☞ Listening and believing negative self-talk
- ☞ Allowing others to dictate your mood
- ☞ Not getting help for emotional pain when you need it
- ☞ Not asking for support
- ☞ Not being open to guidance and direction from appropriate sources

Once you stop sleeping, everything changes. Emotional integrity and healthy life balance lend themselves to good sleep (this used to be called "beauty rest"), and good sleep is the gift that keeps on giving when it comes to other self-care measures, like exercise, healthy eating, and managing stress in healthy ways.

Finding solutions and dealing with what's interfering with good emotional and mental health are key to becoming a Got It Girl.

DOING IT DIFFERENTLY

- ☞ Seek a therapist to help you deal with any difficulties you might be facing.
- ☞ Seek support through other paths, when helpful.

- Try joining a twelve-step group.
- Talk about your feelings with an empathic listener.
- Deal with trauma from your past through psychological work.
- Get support or ask for support when you need it.
- Learn how to tune in to your feelings.
- Recognize what you're feeling, and use that to help you make decisions.
- Detach from others when they are toxic or not helpful.

We have this great survival mechanism—it's called emotions. Emotions have energy, and when we recognize the energy and place value on it, it can be so helpful.

For example, when a woman feels frustrated, this is good information. If she can stop and recognize the annoyed feelings that are bubbling up, if she can notice the tightness in her jaw and the tension in her hands, she can stop and evaluate what's happening. She can ask herself, *Am I allowing some boundaries to be violated? Am I feeling resentful because I am pushing myself too hard on this project? Am I eating well and exercising this week?*

Emotions can be valuable nuggets of wisdom. It's a fine balance, of course: if you are all about your emotions and are overly susceptible to big mood swings, that's not a great place to be.

One of the biggest issues for Giveaway Girls is not recognizing their feelings. For some of you out there, this happens because you have cut yourself off from your feelings for so long that you don't know how to experience or identify them. If this is the case for you, it's important that you learn how to recognize your feelings, name them, and honor them.

By shifting the way you think, you can use your emotions effectively.

SPIRITUALITY

COMMON GIVEAWAY-ISMS

- Looking only to others and yourself for direction, versus relying on spiritual help
- Thinking that you are in control of things you aren't
- Spending time on everything besides connecting with your higher power
- Not setting time aside every day to meditate, pray, sit in silence, or whatever it is that nurtures your spiritual side

Nurturing your soul and your spirituality can go a long way toward helping you shed your Giveaway Girl tendencies. In fact, I have met many women who turned themselves over to their spiritual life for help in facilitating this. It worked! They had tried and tried to do this kind of Got It Girl work completely on their own but had found themselves going back to the beginning, time and time again.

Spiritual sustenance and connection to your higher power is what we all need to help us find our higher self. It is the source of our greatest wisdom and truth. However, in today's go, do, and accomplish society, it doesn't leave room for us to prioritize this path unless we make it so. You can and need to prioritize this, if only to accomplish a life fully lived. The good news is that is a joyful path. Additionally, it is a path that allows you to surrender some major life difficulties for someone else to take care of—for once.

Doing It Differently

- ✎ Use the Serenity Prayer or a similar spiritual belief to help yourself recognize and prioritize peace and discernment in your life.

- ✎ Pray or meditate every day (ideally for at least half an hour, but any time you can set aside is helpful).

- ✎ Meditate, pray, or practice mindfulness when exercising and in other contexts, keeping in mind the importance of creating and maintaining your spiritual/religious connection in your life.

I have a hard time talking about religion and spirituality with others. For me, it is a very quiet and personal relationship and set of beliefs—and beyond that, as a social worker I believe that espousing a certain belief, religion, or spiritual ideal to my clients could be disruptive to their beliefs and harmful to our relationship. Therefore, in my professional life, I keep my own spiritual and religious beliefs to myself and try to honor and learn about those held by the person or persons I am trying to help.

On a personal level, my connection to my higher power is profound. I find strength, direction, peace, and beauty in it. I get bogged down by daily tasks and the go-do-and-accomplish treadmill just like everyone else—but I set aside time each day to pray, meditate, or sit in stillness. I often do so in unexpected places: at the gym, riding in a car, waiting in line at the store. I love the saying "Always find time to spend thirty minutes a day to pray or meditate. If it is a particularly bad day and you cannot spend the time doing this, then increase it to an hour." It's so true.

In order to be successful in your Giveaway Girl recovery—in order to take back who you were really meant to be—you need all the strength and guidance you can get. So if you believe in a Higher Power, ask for help. Accepting your own human limitations will help greatly in your efforts to make changes in your life. For my part, in addition to my religion and my spiritual practices, I belong to a twelve-step group that has substantially helped me to keep myself much healthier and more accountable.

I believe that the twelve steps are a powerful guidance system. This system, combined with the therapeutic strength of a group connection, can sometimes make the impossible possible. Tremendous growth and healing can occur. In addition, twelve-step work helps me stay focused on the important things and loosens the power of the unimportant things. Who doesn't want that?

For those who don't care for religion/spirituality and have no interest in it, there are still benefits to spending time in quiet reflection and mindfulness. Powerful research supports the benefits of Transcendental Meditation as a tool for coping and healing.[10] It has been proven to counter medical problems, elevate one's mood, and promote overall wellness. I highly recommend it. Yoga is another powerful tool you can use.

I have a mentor, Arlene Englander, who wrote the book *The In-Sourcing Handbook: Where and How to Find the Happiness You Deserve*, which features myriad quick and easy insights and exercises that help promote self-care.[11] The following is a meditation practice Arlene taught me. I find it extremely helpful at promoting wisdom and insight when I am overwhelmed or perplexed. I call it my Golden Light Visualization.

GOLDEN LIGHT VISUALIZATION

---

1. Start out by breathing deeply through your nose, in for eight seconds; hold for four; then breathe out for eight.

2. After you have done this about eight to ten times, picture yourself firmly rooted by a golden cord that connects you to the earth.

3. In your mind's eye, connect your mind with a golden light to the sky, the universe, and the source of infinite wisdom.

4. Once your mind is connected, then visualize your heart connecting. The mind and the heart have to be connected to each other and then connected to the sky in a circular chain.

I like to visualize a circular golden light that connects my mind with my heart, my heart with my mind, and then goes straight up through the top of my head, from which it connects upward to the source of my higher power.

Interestingly, you can feel this powerful, warm force. Stay with this while still breathing, and just feel it. Remember, your intention is wisdom and light. Try to keep all other thoughts away for just this time. Be on the lookout for clarity to come later. It works for me.

You can find numerous relaxation and meditation exercises on YouTube. Go for it. Just make room in your life for this.

Personally, I just do my best to prioritize time for this every day, and I don't beat up on myself if it doesn't happen. Tomorrow is another day. I will say that I feel such a difference in energy, optimism, and perspective on days when I make this a priority. This is motivating enough.

On Addiction

c◉

Addiction is so prevalent in our society. Clearly, there are powerful emotional, physiological and neurological components to this epidemic, but I am one of those therapists who believe that addiction in all forms is an attempt to escape our negative feelings. It's a natural human inclination—and it can lead us down a very bad road.

Addictions can be a self-sabotaging manner of coping, which is why so many Giveaway Girls become addicted to alcohol or prescription or illegal drugs, as well as to shopping, eating, hoarding, gambling, and sexual addiction. Interestingly, I have even seen many Giveaway Girls become addicted to the high they get from self-neglect.

If you think you may be addicted—to anything— you need to get help. No one can break free from an addiction completely on her own; it just doesn't work that way. The same goes for you if you're in a relationship with an addict. You cannot take care of yourself within this relationship without help, guidance, and support. So take care of yourself by reaching out to a therapist or enrolling in a twelve-step or treatment program.

c◉

MORE ON SELF-CARE:
QUESTIONS TO ASK YOURSELF

PROFESSIONALLY

Are you challenging yourself professionally? Are you working toward following your dreams of the perfect job? Even if you are on hiatus or working at a job you don't like, it is possible to invent special projects or secretly work on the best résumé in history while you wait. Whether we are stay-at-home moms, fast-food workers, nurses, teachers, or corporate executives, we all have something we're naturally good at, in addition to our profession. Use your natural gifts and intellect to their best advantage.

ARTISTICALLY

What are you doing to indulge your creative side? Are you painting, drawing, or decorating your house? Even arranging flowers on a beautiful day is a creative outlet. Your creative energy is inside you, and it's bursting to get out. If you don't indulge it, it can lead to anxiety, discomfort, and negative energy. If you need inspiration, check out Julia Cameron's *The Artist's Way*.

AESTHETICALLY

Do you allow yourself to indulge in beauty for the fun of it? This could mean making sure your house is decorated beautifully or putting together a lovely outfit. It could mean having your toenails painted a color that makes you smile or going for a walk in a pretty place. It can be anything, really, as long as it stimulates your appreciation for the beauty around you.

I have a friend who complained about the dullness of her living room curtains for three years and yet did nothing to change them. She was not taking care of herself. I confronted her about her inaction, and together we found some gorgeous purple silk curtains that were within her budget. It made her so happy—and it was so easy to accomplish!

MY TOP TEN ADDITIONS TO YOUR SELF-CARE AGENDA

---

1. Laughter. I laugh a lot. I laugh at myself even when things seem dire. Try it. It will make you feel better, I promise.

2. Compassion. Please have compassion for yourself. You are learning and growing and doing your best every day with the information you have at the time. Everybody has setbacks. Be empathetic with yourself and try, try again.

3. Forgiveness. Forgive yourself for not doing everything perfectly in the time and manner you want. You are only human. Each and every time you screw up, forgive yourself and move on.

4. Kindness in your self-talk. So important. Negative self-talk, as Rick Carson points out in his book *Taming Your Gremlin,* is like an evil gremlin that sabotages you at every turn. Recognize when you are allowing your inner critic to take over, and try to reframe your self-talk to be more encouraging and accepting.

5. Spiritual practice. Praying, meditating, or connecting with your spiritual self in whatever way makes sense

to you will help you on your journey toward self-care (even five minutes a day). Very important!

6. Vulnerability. Nobody's perfect—and neither are you. Our imperfections are what make us unique and interesting. Embrace them!

7. Know self-neglect can be addictive. Remember this.

8. Self-love. Treat yourself as you would treat your best friend.

9. You are valuable. Imagine yourself as a beautiful gift, all wrapped in paper, with a gorgeous bow on top! I usually like to imagine myself wrapped in that Tiffany blue with a white satin bow on top. Doing this makes me smile.

10. What makes you happy? If you are thinking about buying something or doing something that will make you happy and you can afford it, do it! A lot of Giveaway Girls can afford good things for themselves, but they allow their unearned guilt to hold them back. Buy it or do it for yourself. You have nothing to feel guilty about.

Baby Steps

If you do nothing else after reading this book besides starting to take care of yourself a little better, then writing this book was worth it—because once you start actively trying to treat yourself better, your life will change for the better! But remember: it isn't enough simply to take a theoretical approach to caretaking; you must make it operational. Just do it.

It's okay if the motivation and feeling good about it don't immediately travel from your head into your heart. Motivation often comes after you have already engaged in a behavior. If you're feeling overwhelmed by all the things you need to do or change in order to improve your self-care, just pick one thing and work on it for a few weeks. There's no need for a mad rush to do it all in one day. That is just setting yourself up for failure (which is not good self-care!).

Ever cleaned a bathroom grudgingly and then started feeling zippier by the time you finished spraying the Windex? Then you got into it and had more energy to finish? Same principle here. The more self-care you practice, the more you'll want to practice. Feeling good feels good!

CHAPTER 10

✑

LETTING GO WHEN IT'S HARD TO LET GO

"How much easier is self-sacrifice than self-realization."

—ERIC HOFFER

L etting go of detrimental caretaking won't be easy. We have established that. Before we summarize Getting It Back in Chapter 11, we first need to be honest within ourselves. There's a dirty little secret among us Giveaway Girls: the secret is that there are some upsides to staying stuck in detrimental caretaking mode.

THERE'S AN UPSIDE TO STAYING STUCK?

Oh yeah—any behavior, even one that is unhealthy or bad for us, has some upsides. These upsides are a big part of how we stay stuck. For example, people smoke, overeat, drink too much, and engage in other unhealthy behaviors partly because they are getting pleasure, relief, a buzz, or some sort of positive from it. We therapists call this the secondary gain. In mental health–speak, this theory claims that a basic psychological truth for all humans is that we don't consistently behave in a certain way unless we are getting something from it.

At times, those upsides seem to feel better than getting to the other side of that unhealthy behavior. Therefore, in order to get unstuck from detrimental caretaking, you have to figure out what your secondary gains are. Be honest with yourself. What could you be getting from giving it away? Which of these secondary gains can you relate to?

FIVE SECONDARY GAINS OF DETRIMENTAL CARETAKING

----

1. Control helps you feel secure.
2. Self-pity feels good.
3. It's what you know.
4. You have an excuse to act badly.
5. You don't have to face your fears.

Before we explore these secondary gains, please understand that they are usually unconscious and unintentional. Most Giveaway Girls don't do this stuff while they are aware of it. That is why we are exploring these feelings here.

Detrimental caretaking is primarily a learned behavior and a way of coping that has evolved. So, as I give these examples, understand and have compassion for yourself and for the women you know who do this. It is okay to laugh at yourself too if you recognize yourself in any of these examples. I know I have found myself in victim territory a time or two in my life. There are so many reasons for this. Read on!

SECONDARY GAIN #1

Control Helps You Feel Secure

Are you a controller? Many Giveaway Girls have a strong need to control. Why else would they jump into the fray and take on all the responsibilities for someone else? If they have to do it, it will at least get it done their way and the way they want.

Getting things done the "right way" feels extremely important to many Giveaway Girls. Many want to be in charge, they want to make things happen as they see fit, or they complain about "always having to be in charge," but they won't let go of responsibility when they could. It is hard to give up controlling desires.

FIX, MANAGE, AND CONTROL

Michelle is like that in her household and at work. She runs her department like a well-oiled machine. She is always at the hospital, helping to fill in the gaps and taking care of everything before anyone can realize what is needed. Although Michelle displays a wonderful work ethic, she is camouflaging a need to control that extends from her job to her home.

If Michelle's kids have a problem, she does whatever she can to fix it. When her daughter was struggling with friend drama and hurt feelings, Michelle stepped in and called the other girl's mother to work it out. Michelle's secondary gain is feeling like she can fix, manage, and control things. This gives her a better sense of security.

The need to control comes from a Giveaway Girl's feeling out of control to begin with. Fear and anxiety within get stirred up easily, so controlling can feel like a reasonable antidote.

True serenity comes from knowing we have very little control over the world around us.

Ever Heard the Serenity Prayer?

God, grant me the serenity to accept the things I cannot change
The courage to change the things I can,
And help me let go of the things I can't,
and give me the wisdom to know the difference.

What is great about no longer giving it away is that you become more empowered and more in control of the things you can control and less entrenched in trying to control things you can't. Think of your hands tightly grasping the steering wheel of a boat in a tempest, except the wheel isn't even connected to the rudder. Sure, it feels good to do something, except you are exerting energy and stress needlessly.

Feeling as if you are controlling something is a powerful motivator for staying stuck in the Giveaway Girl way of life.

Secondary Gain #2

Self-Pity Feels Good

Detrimental caretakers tend to be self-pity partiers. Having a pity party and feeling really bad is absolutely all right. We need this sometimes. It is a part of the human condition, especially when we are feeling great loss, sadness, hurt, or grief. Self-pity can seem soothing and useful; however, when we don't have healthier ways to cope and don't feel empowered, we can get to where we stay in this mode instead of attempting to change our circumstances.

How is it that too much self-pity can be attractive? Well, lots of reasons. You can feel sorry for yourself. You can even feel righteous and indignant. You can feel as if you are the one who has been wronged and taken advantage of. You can wallow in self-pity. In a weird way, self-pity can feel good.

The problem with too much self-pity is that it is a rut that gets deeper with the time and effort you put into it. Your self-pity is hard for other people to deal with, too. Self-pity, like any other bad habit, can be broken. If you are someone who can't stop the self-pity, turn that negative energy around and use it to accomplish something. An individual counselor or coach can help.

There comes a time in our lives to stop the self-pity. Giveaway Girls can find it hard to let go.

BENEFITS OF THE VICTIM/MARTYR MINDSET

Women have rightfully found a place for themselves in victimhood. Given how they have been treated historically, and sometimes are treated even now, this makes sense.

Martyrdom was especially useful in the past: when women were forced into marriages and unable to own land; when abuse against a woman was considered a man's right (in some countries, it still is). Maybe back then this martyr/victim mentality served a purpose. A woman could feel righteous, indignant, and proud of her ability to stoically tolerate mal-treatment. Maybe it gave her a sense that there was something noble in the situation—a situation that made her suffering and sacrifice important, or "worth it."

Women in the late 1950s, '60s, and maybe even '70s had significantly fewer powerful roles than women do today. So it should be no wonder how victimization can become deeply rooted in the emotional style of so many women.

Nowadays, women lead different lives and have more options than in generations past—different lives, more options, and a whole wide world of possibilities!

Remember what I said in Chapter 6 about Giveaway Girls sometimes coming from mothers who were Giveaway Girls?

Many mothers before us showed us a victim-like mentality. They were taught disempowerment and allowed to be only victims—taught to do as they were told, to smile and go along. And they did. They had to.

It can be difficult to see that you always have choices in life, no matter how tough a situation. For the women martyrs in history, no one told them or showed them this possibility. The following are a few ways in which the victim/martyr mindset feels good.

1. I Am So Noble

There is definite nobility in important and necessary self-sacrifice: a mother who gives her last ounce of energy to finish her day at work so she can get a paycheck; a father who turns down a promotion because he knows it would mean moving his family at a difficult time; a friend who shares his lunch with his best friend.

We are blessed to live in a society full of shining examples of humanitarian giving and honoring God's wish that "we give unto others." But Giveaway Girls can sometimes choose this route over and over again unnecessarily.

If you are victimizing yourself, think through that decision. Ask yourself, *Will it truly make a difference?* Is it coming from a darker place, like your ego or a desire simply to feel significant in the world?

2. I Am So Needed and Necessary

Victimhood feels good because it feeds a false sense of importance. The worker bee who overfunctions to the point of exhaustion does so because it feels good to feel that important.

You can feel needed and necessary: "What would they do without you?" This also applies to the mom who can't tear herself away from her family for some girl time. (Why does her husband keep texting her, when she's been gone for only an hour?) She is loving the feeling of being needed, even though this is not the reality.

The bad news and the good news is that the rest of the world (even your kids) would do just fine without your detrimental caretaking. In fact, they would get opportunities to use their strengths; they could learn and grow. The Giveaway Girl gets enormous glee from thinking she is the cog in the wheel that makes the wagon turn. Giveaway Girl, there are much healthier ways to feel good that don't involve your depletion. (But, oooh, it can feel good!)

3. I Am So Important

You are not that important. You may run around overfunctioning and overdoing because you think the world will end if you don't. I hate to break it to you, but the truth is that the world will not end if you stop doing all of those things you do.

Everyone wants to feel important and special in some way. Detrimental caretaking can make us feel this way. It's not real, though; it is our ego telling us that we are vital and important because of our self-sacrifice.

Let's picture the story of Sally to explain this point.

Sally, a woman in her late seventies, was upset and overwhelmed about her adult son's meth addiction. He was in his late thirties, and Sally was supporting him and his girlfriend. Sally paid the rent, paid for his BMW, and bailed him out of jail several times. This freed Sally's son to use whatever economic resources he could find to feed his drug problem. He occasionally robbed Sally and brought horribly dangerous people to her door.

Sally was stuck partially because this "helping" made her feel important. As painful as her son's drug addiction was to watch, she felt vital to his life. She had no idea she was enabling him. She would have been horrified at the thought. After all, she loved him desperately.

What Sally didn't see about herself was that by staying stuck in this victim role, she was feeding a need to be a necessary and active part of his life—even if it was the meth part. Sally's son was thankful and appreciative of all that she gave him. She believed her "support" was meaningful. Meanwhile, Sally didn't go to therapy and couldn't find the time to attend a twelve-step group that could help her free herself from this role. She told herself she just didn't have the time or the money, when what she was really struggling with was letting go of her victimhood and this feeling of importance.

4. Blaming Others Is Easier

Another tempting way to feel good about being a victim is by playing the blame game. That is when we accept that we cannot achieve or do better, or that we have to stay stuck and suffer because of external forces.

Giveaway Girls can blame their life circumstances from early on; they could choose to blame their mean or oppressive husbands or partners. They could choose the bad bosses they have had; they could choose how they are treated by their family. Some Giveaway Girls could choose to blame the system for their lack of financial power. (And, as I have said before, some women, especially minority women, do have less access to financial and political power.) One could rest on that. Any and all of these excuses are powerful for the Giveaway Girl.

Blaming gets attention. It wastes time and distracts us from changing. Blaming others means you are moving backward, not forward, dealing with the present by staying stuck in the past.

SECONDARY GAIN #3

It's What You Know

Familiarity feels comfortable. We are more inclined to take the path that is well worn, the one we know well. Forging a new path in untested territory brings up confusion, anxiety, and discomfort. It can cause disruptions from our norm. We don't want things to be different, even if things will be better.

CHANGE IS HARD

You might remember the 1998 best-selling book about change, entitled *Who Moved My Cheese?*, by Spencer Johnson.[1] It tells the story of some mice in a maze whose cheese gets moved around. They don't like it. Some adapt and decide to overcome their fears and the upset of losing control. Others resist and refuse to budge.

Copious research concludes that resistance to change is common.[2] When you make changes, you will sense resistance from others. People just want things to continue the way they were, even if it is not good for them or for you. We will talk more about system resistance in the last chapter.

HABITS ARE HARD TO BREAK

People don't want to budge from what they have going on. Studies show that the average time for a new behavior to reach

peak automaticity is sixty-six days.[3] That is only one behavior change that has to be repeated on a daily basis. That's a
whole lot of effort. No wonder we want to keep doing what
we're doing.

WE DO WHAT WE SEE

Many of us were parented by Giveaway Girls or Giveaway
Guys. Pretty much all studies out there about child development assert that children want to model the behaviors of their
parents.[4] The magnitude of this dynamic should not be lost
on Giveaway Girls. Those women were our models and
teachers. You tend to do what you see. Much of what was
modeled was useful. Your job is to modify what wasn't.

Trauma

*It is important that I restate that trauma, and having
experienced trauma, makes the experience of victimization a familiar one. In no way am I asserting that
victims want to be victimized. This is as ridiculous as
saying women want to be beaten. However, trauma
has a way of wanting to resolve itself. Trauma can
feel, almost imperceptibly, like "something you know or
something that is familiar." We are drawn to what is
familiar—whether it is good or bad.*

*In addition, it is not uncommon for victims of
trauma to have difficulty recognizing trauma when it
happens again. I call it the boiling-frog syndrome. You
may have heard this urban myth: you put a frog in a slow-
boiling pot, and he doesn't jump out until it's too late.*

> *Trauma victims have understandably experienced tremendous pain, which makes it harder for trauma victims to recognize when they are in trouble. Previous trauma makes it harder for them to know how to get out of those situations, because of a phenomenon called learned helplessness. But going from survivor to thriver is absolutely possible. Part of that shift has to include moving away from the victim role.*
>
> ◦◦

SECONDARY GAIN #4

You Have an Excuse to Act Badly

Giveaway Girls are wonderful, caring people. For that reason, they have to use an excuse to act badly. We can't just act out poorly for no reason. We Giveaway Girls have to disguise it from ourselves and cushion our bad behavior.

Giveaway Girls who engage in this negative stuff are usually not consciously aware of the harm they are doing. They intend no harm by guilting people or trying to control them. That is why it is so important to talk about this, to locate it within your awareness, so you can recognize it in yourself and others when you come across it. See if you recognize any parts of you in here, or in any Giveaway Girls you know.

LAYING GUILT TRIPS

Guilting is when you use guilt to try to get people to do what you want. I once had a client whose mother had a script she'd use on her every time she called: "Oh, honey, I am so glad you called. I thought you might be dead, it's been so long." Instead of asking for her daughter to call, this mom tried to use guilt to get her way or to share her displeasure. Inside, her mother was frightened and overwhelmed at having to ask for her needs to be met. In addition, she never knew she could or should ask for her needs to be met more directly and respectfully. Using guilt was all she knew, and it was effective in the short run.

CROSS-DRAGGING

Another way to try to control other people and get them to do what you want sounds somewhat similar to the laying-guilt-trips example. However, cross-dragging is when you act as if you are the one who has been hurt or harmed by someone else's behavior. Then you try to use their feeling guilty and responsible for your pain as a way to get what you want. (Again, this is totally not a conscious thing and not something that all Giveaway Girls do.)

Bernice was a cross-dragger for much of her life. On her birthday, she really wanted her friends to do something for her, but instead of asking, she talked about how depressing her birthday would be by herself and how she couldn't stand the idea of spending another special day all alone, indulging in a quart of Häagen-Dazs. She would just curl up with a big sigh. Call out: If you are a big sigher, you just may be a Giveaway Girl!

People feel sorry for those who suffer, and they tend to want to do something about it. Sadly, this was how Bernice had always gotten her needs met. And Bernice believes (as I said in Chapter 4 when I talked about being honest and direct) that she shouldn't have to ask, but hinting isn't helpful. It is hard to give up the ways in which we get our needs met. I understand, Bernice.

HAVING IT YOUR WAY

Another secondary gain for Giveaway Girl behavior is that by overfunctioning, not letting go of control, and changing for the positive, we can call all the shots. Sara has always been the overfunctioner in her company and with her family. She knows what to do and how to do it. Everybody relies on her.

At family events, everybody gives Sara the money and expects her to order the food, organize the meeting place, and take care of all the arrangements. Sara hates this. However, if she steps away from this role, Sara will have to accept somebody else's opinions, preferences, and choices. There is where detrimental caretaking has its payoffs: Sara doesn't really want to give up her top-dog role.

JUDGING OTHERS

It is so easy to judge others, to feel like we know the right way and the wrong way to do and be. Some Giveaway Girls are really into this, probably because they are their own worst critics. They are harder on themselves than anyone! Some Giveaway Girls get secondary gains from the mind frame that they have the right to interfere, judge, and tell people what to do. It is like the caretaking tendency has given them carte blanche to "help" anyone whom they see as "needing" their help.

Mind Your Own Business (MYOB)

⌒∽

The harsh Giveaway Girl reality is that no one should get your advice unless they ask for it, and then you can tell them only once. Otherwise, you are trying to push your agenda or control the outcome. In addition, if they do or don't follow your advice, that is their choice. If you are mad about it, you are trying to control them. Stopping detrimental caretaking means you have to MYOB.

Changing your life and embracing healthier self-care means you have to let go of interfering in other people's business and step away from trying to control others. The upside to change? You will have the time and energy to work on the real person needing the knowledge, grace, and wisdom—you!

⌒∽

SECONDARY GAIN #5
You Don't Have to Face Your Fears

Facing your fears and making changes is scary. Being a Giveaway Girl can feel comfortable, like an old sweatshirt that you put on when it is cold—no need to face fears or get out there and challenge yourself. Just stay stuck. Fear can be so powerful. Remember what I said about the subtle fear implications that we women are messaged a lot of the time? That doesn't help.

Eleanor Roosevelt once said, "We gain strength, and courage, and confidence by each experience in which we really stop to look fear in the face . . . . We must do that which we think we cannot."

HIDING IN YOUR CAVE

Sometimes people feel too afraid of making changes. In the short term, it can be easier to hide behind a bad relationship, a bad job, or a bad lifestyle than it is to make different choices. A lot of people stay in bad marriages because they are afraid to do the things they need to do by themselves. They don't want to face the world as a single person or parent. They are overwhelmed at the idea of taking care of themselves, so they choose to remain stuck and disempowered. This is certainly not the case in all bad relationships, but it rings true for some. Using victimization can feel like a shield, even though it isn't.

Most people are doing the best they can with where they are in life and with the tools they have. You might find yourself in this group. That is totally okay. It is understandable to be fearful and to want to stay in your cave for a while. You will make the changes when the time is right for you. There is no major rush, Giveaway Girl. I just want you to do some inner looking to see what might be holding you back.

PREPARING TO FACE YOUR FEARS

Not being a victim means facing your fears. You may not even completely know what you are afraid of.

You are facing your fears just by reading this book. I commend you for that. It can seem easier to feed fears and not push forward. However, agreeing with and abiding your fears, while you stay stuck, is a life not fully lived. You get to decide what you want and need in your life. I am confident that you will do your best and succeed. Facing your fears will make all the difference!

Step 1: Know what you're afraid of.

I read this from Martha Beck, who writes for *O, the Oprah Magazine*. She always has something useful and enlightening to say.[5] Martha suggests this fill-in-the-blank exercise.

1. I want .... in my life.
   But I am afraid of ....

2. I want .... in my life.
   But I am afraid of ....

3. I want .... in my life.
   But I am afraid of ....

4. I want .... in my life.
   But I am afraid of ....

5. I want .... in my life.
   But I am afraid of ....

6. I want .... in my life.
   But I am afraid of ....

Personally, I find that when I am feeling fearful or anxious, I make myself say out loud exactly what I am afraid of. I keep saying every possible thing I might be fearing. What is nice about that is that when you hear yourself say things out loud, sometimes they lose their power. It takes the pent-up fear energy that is inside us and releases it. Once in a while, I laugh at the ridiculousness of some of my fears. Then I can smile and move on.

Step 2: Feel the fear and take a step anyway.

Accept that you will feel uncomfortable. This is an important life truth. Now, I am not saying you should do *everything* you are afraid of. Some fears are useful. They keep us from taking a weird drug that a stranger tries selling us on the streets of Thailand. (You know what I mean.)

Step 3: Take baby steps.

Don't do anything huge overnight. This will be too big a shock, and too hard. Just put your toe in the pool. Sit for a while. Then make yourself take another step.

Step 4: Get support.

You will need it. A therapist, best friend, rabbi or minister, or twelve-step group can help. The more support you have, the better. I have been blessed and honored to see my clients accomplish remarkable things when they have been supported and encouraged. You can do it, too. Rely on the guidance, strength, experience, and faith of others when you don't feel like you have enough of your own. Stay the course. Join the Stop Giving It Away blog [www.stopgivingitaway.com] and connect with other women on the same quest!

CLAIM YOUR SPACE, POWER, AND HAPPINESS

I know it isn't easy. Sometimes the aftermath of trauma, broken and dysfunctional relationships, and past disappointments combines with societal pressures and adds to the mountain of fear inside you. These feelings can overwhelm you and compete with your willingness to overcome. Try not to wait for the fear to lessen, but to reach and pray for your strength to help you feel primed for the task.

Remember back in Chapter 1 when I told you about that field, the one you were required to walk through? You couldn't run through it freely, stopping to pick the wildflowers—you were stuck on a path, bound in by thorny bushes and thick vegetation on either side. You couldn't see the branches hemming you in; you could only feel them.

The time has come to make a fresh start. You now understand the invisible forces holding you back. You are practicing setting boundaries and enforcing them. You are speaking up and out for your wants and needs. You are starting to see some of your dreams, hopes, and desires get closer. Soon, the field that is your life will be wide open for you to live well and enjoy.

Don't wait until you are no longer afraid. Your space, power, and happiness are yours to claim. I am here to help. Next, seven steps to getting it back.

CHAPTER 11

⊷

CALL TO ACTION:
SEVEN STEPS TO GETTING IT BACK

"To create more positive results in your life,
replace 'if only' with 'next time.'"
—CELESTINE CHUA

Based on the success I've had with transforming my Giveaway Girl clients into Got It Girls, I've outlined a seven-step progression that will take you from surviving to thriving. Some of it is a review of what you have already read, but I find it's helpful to have a single list to refer to. The seven steps are as follows:

1. Recognize there is a problem.

2. Identify the dynamics that have caused these issues to flourish in your life.

3. Establish what you can do to realign your life and set boundaries.

4. Set those boundaries.

5. Take care of yourself.

6. Manage your guilt.

7. Put together a relapse plan.

Let's explore each of these steps a little more in-depth.

STEP 1

Recognize there is a problem.

You're already halfway there: you bought this book and you read it, and therefore you are probably ready to knock the first step off the list. If you're going to become a Got It Girl, you need to make sure you have 100-percent accepted that you're currently a Giveaway Girl. Why?

Let me put it this way: the military spends millions of dollars every year making sure battle clothing is colored and textured to fit into the environment where the soldiers are heading. The military doesn't do this for fun; it does so because camouflage works! It allows the military to take something foreign and make it look like a natural part of the surrounding environment.

Throughout this book, we have discussed how religion, culture, gender expectations and values, and our early, formative experiences lead so many of us to make unhealthy self-sacrifices and engage in detrimental caretaking with others. These systems camouflage what is really going on so that these behavior patterns can be perpetuated; they hide the enemy. That's why active recognition is so important: identifying and acknowledging our tendency to give it away is the most important step we can take toward changing it.

STEP 2

Identify the dynamics that have caused these issues to flourish in your life.

Now that you understand how your Giveaway Girl identity formed, it is important to be clear about which dynamics within your life are allowing (or causing) these issues to continue to flourish. Here are some questions to ask yourself in order to single out these dynamics:

- What is going on in your life, and within your decision making, that will inhibit your making changes in your life?
- How did you become a Giveaway Girl?
- What early experiences may have contributed to your becoming a detrimental caretaker?
- Have you been impacted by addiction?
- What aspects of being a detrimental caretaker have been useful for you?
- What aspects of detrimental caretaking have hindered and hurt your success and happiness in life?
- What might you have picked up from your culture regarding self-sacrifice? From your family?
- What do you want to change about your life?
- What is it about your personality or who you believe yourself to be that makes it difficult for you to set boundaries or take care of yourself?
- What different choices would you like to start making?
- How would you rather your life look?

Visualization Exercise

♥

Take a minute to visualize yourself acting differently in a situation in which you frequently find yourself. Pick a scenario where you normally give it away, shut your eyes, and picture yourself behaving and acting differently than you normally do. Try to visualize as much detail as possible, as if it were playing on a screen in front of you, like a movie.

For example, if your boss often comes at you with demands and indiscriminate requests and you want to react more confidently, you might think of a canned response you could use: "One request at a time, John. Wait until I have a pen." Remember to envision yourself saying it with a confident voice while standing tall and assuming an assertive posture (i.e., not standing with your arms crossed and your head hanging). If you behave more passively at work than you would like, this could be a great exercise for you.

If it is in your personal relationships that you would like to feel more empowered, try visualizing a scenario for that: for example, maybe you could imagine kindly telling your partner that you are making some changes and are going to need them to step up to the plate more. Whatever the scenario, make sure you include in your visualization the feelings of pride, confidence, respect, and happiness that go with standing up for yourself. Again, focus on your body language.

If you're having too much trouble imagining yourself being so assertive, try envisioning someone whom you admire doing it, and then imagine stepping into their body and seeing things through their eyes. Sit with that a bit. Eventually, you'll be able to see yourself doing it—and then you will do it!

◦◉

STEP 3

Establish what you can do to realign your life and set boundaries.

Get a notepad and answer the following questions:

◦◉ What are the current problems or issues where you currently spend most of your time and energy?

◦◉ What do you feel you "have to do" each day, each week, each month that gets in the way of what is most important to you (for example: work, cleaning house, carpooling, cooking, extra projects)?

◦◉ What would you really like to spend your time and energy doing? Are there things you wish you could spend more time on or give more of your attention to? If you had only one year to live, what are some things you would want to experience and accomplish?

I work through this exercise one-on-one with my clients, and I've found it especially helpful. One client showed me so many ways in which she used her energy each day that she ran out of room on the page for what she wanted for herself. Imagine: no space left for what she wanted and needed. It was one of those "aha" moments for her. We decided to do a Conscious Calendar for her and it really helped her learn to prioritize her needs in a healthier way.

Surprised by how little time you're spending on the things you *want* to do? Sad that your days are filled with things you'd rather not be spending your energy on? Consider this a wake-up call. The whole idea of this exercise is to show you that you need to clear space for the fun stuff. All those "little, everyday" sacrifices add up in terms of time and energy—perhaps more than you realize.

THE CONSCIOUS CALENDAR

To keep "have-tos" and "shoulds" from crowding out your "want-tos," sit down at the beginning of each week to schedule in your self-care and hopes and dreams for the next seven days. Put those in the calendar *first* (even if only in fifteen-minute increments), and then fill in the rest of your schedule. Otherwise, the have-tos and shoulds will just shove those want-tos out of the way, like a bully would to the smallest kid in the lunch line.

STEP 4

Set those boundaries.

Go back to Chapter 8 and review those boundary rules and the list of weapons of mass detriment.

Memory refreshed? Good. Now let's go over a quick pros-and-cons list regarding setting boundaries.

SETTING BOUNDARIES: PROS

- You will feel better.
- You will get your life back.
- You will be less tense.
- You will get your needs met.
- You will die a happy person. (Okay, I can't guarantee this last one, but it sounds good, doesn't it?)

SETTING BOUNDARIES: CONS

- Some people will get mad at first.
- Initially you will feel worse than when you didn't set boundaries, because of unearned guilt, extra pressure, and social brainwashing.
- If you set a hard boundary, you have to follow through on it—and that can be pretty difficult.

Start small when you begin setting boundaries. Don't set yourself up to fail by taking on too much at once! Don't go in with your bat swinging, either. Remember, you might have some pent-up codependent rage, and you don't want to take things out on the people around you. Go slow and easy, and you'll be just fine.

STEP 5

Take care of yourself.

If you aren't making big changes in how you take care of yourself (i.e., if you're still not taking care of yourself), it's unlikely that you'll be able to sustain the other positive changes in your life. This step has to happen. Just like they always tell you on airplanes, you have to secure your own air mask before doing anything else.

Some pros and cons of taking better care of yourself:

TAKING CARE OF YOURSELF: PROS

- You will feel better.
- You will be stronger, better nourished, and better able to do what you need to do to get your life back.
- You will be less tense.
- You will start feeling more valuable, and that will enhance all aspects of your life.
- You will serve as a model for others, who will be inspired by the changes you've made.
- You will begin to live the life you were meant to live.

TAKING CARE OF YOURSELF: CONS

- This might at first not appeal to you. (Boring!)
- You have to do some things you don't want to do and stop doing some things you don't want to stop doing.
- It takes effort.
- In the short term, it may feel better to ignore your needs than to address them (refer again to Chapter 10).
- Self-neglect can be addicting.
- Learning something new can be intimidating.
- You may feel some resistance against these changes, because they go against how you have always lived.

⋴ Your partner or friends may overtly or covertly influence you to stay in those old ways that were not (and still are not) good for you.

STEP 6

Manage your guilt.

Guilt ranks as the number-one reason women find it so hard to take care of themselves. They feel guilty and bad when they disappoint others by saying no or bowing out of things that they feel that they "should" do, so, to avoid that feeling, they simply say yes—even when they don't want to.

First of all, let's just acknowledge that framing anything as a "should" is guilt-inducing. By using "should" statements, either with others or even just in your own head, you are really tyin' on a big bag of guilt. Why do that to yourself?

Guilt arises from shame, which is one of what I call the "big five" emotions—along with anger, sadness, happiness/joy, and fear. Shame ranks as the worst of the five, or at least as a runner-up to fear. And usually, the guilt that comes from this shame is unearned. Let me repeat: the guilt you feel is almost always unearned.

Recall what we've covered about the institutional, cultural, and religious pressures that have taught you what your role in life should be. Very powerful! As a woman, you are viewed in many ways as a second-class citizen. (If you're a minority woman out there, you might want to make it third- or fourth-class.)

Individual experiences and family roles add to these pressures as well. If you've come from a dysfunctional family, guilt and shame will be major players in the formation of your concept of self. Abuse and addiction just add to the heap.

When you try to move away from these roles or ideas, the first thing you're likely to feel is guilt. That guilt, though powerful, has no real basis—and it serves only to keep you stuck.

I used to work with a client who was very active in a twelve-step group. One day, she told me what her sponsor had said to her about managing the kind of guilt I'm talking about, and I thought it was brilliant: "Look," she told her, "you can't make the feelings of unearned guilt and shame go away. The only way to make them disappear is by making the tough choices you need to make to be okay in your life. Then you just have to accept that you are going to feel guilty . . . and do it anyway! Because your other option is worse. Your only other option is to do what makes you not feel guilty: saying yes when you want to say no. Doing the things you don't want to do. But what that does is breed resentment. And that resentment and anger will build and build, nothing will change, and you'll blow your lid (or blow someone else's lid). And then what? You still have to change anyway. Except now you've wasted your time, wasted other people's time, and created chaos and resentment, which makes you feel guilty and mad—and you're still stuck right back where you started."

In other words, saying yes to chairing the committee because you feel guilty, then getting mad when no one else steps up, is a recipe for disaster. You get mad and say you'll never work with so-and-so again; you act bitchy and mean to your partner and children; you lose sleep and begin feeling tired all the time. Maybe, after feeling like this for a while, you seek out some support and start dealing with your guilt and trying to base your decisions on what's best for you. What if you had decided to decline the invitation in the first place? What if you had simply said, "That won't work for me" and left it at that? What would have been better? What do you think?

My Giveaway Girl clients tell me it takes tremendous courage to face their guilt and set the limits they know work for them. However, they also tell me that the more they do it, the easier it becomes. As with any new skill, you must practice it repeatedly in order to build confidence in your abilities.

With some clients, I recommend using the "will anyone die" technique—in other words, I tell them to ask themselves, *Will anyone die if I* ....*?* It's a great way to put your guilt in perspective when that guilt becomes paralyzing and scary. If no one's going to die, then it's probably okay.

You're at a fork in the road, Giveaway Girl. One decision is better for you at this point in your life, and you know it—but you feel guilty. It's easier for Giveaway Girls to take the path of least resistance (or less guilt) and just give it away. But is that going to work forever? Do you really want to live that way?

Manage your guilt and get support.

STEP 7

Put together a relapse plan.

Now that you have a clearer idea of the changes you need to make in your life, make sure you formulate a relapse plan. That's right. Expect that you may fall back into old behaviors and reactions and get back into hurtful patterns. It is okay if this happens. Changing your behavior is one of the most difficult things you can do, and the likelihood that you will begin to behave exactly the way you want to behave after the first try is very, very slim. Don't expect to get a 100 percent your first day out—even if you are the kind of woman who usually excels at everything.

When you do backslide, the best thing you can do is acknowledge that it's happening. Once you've done that, it is helpful to keep two things in mind: 1) recovery requires support; and 2) recovery is a process. Let's spend a little time with each of these concepts.

RECOVERY REQUIRES SUPPORT.

Remember what I said about how when you set boundaries and make changes, everyone will resist, some people will get angry, and things will go berserk for a while? Well, if I haven't mentioned it yet, let me do that now. System resistance makes it so that when one person changes, the whole system feels threatened. Just notice how freaked out everybody gets when the government makes big changes. That isn't even as threatening as something that affects our personal world. So expect some strong reactions when you start implementing the strategies you've learned here. My advice is to simply grab your surfboard and ride the waves. Everyone will adjust eventually—but until then, it may be a bumpy ride.

With that in mind, remember that you can't do this all on your own. You can try, of course (and Giveaway Girls love to think they can do *everything* themselves), but ultimately, you're going to need others to support and lift you up along the way, especially since there will be others trying to drag you down.

What kind of support you seek out is up to you. Your relapse plan could include the formal use of professionals, a self-advocacy coach, a support group, support blog or a therapist and/or work mentor; it could involve trying out a free, confidential twelve-step program; or you could simply team up with a girlfriend whom you can call and check in with about your progress on a weekly basis. (Keep in mind that these aren't either/or options; you can do them all, if you want to.)

Whatever support system you create for yourself, remember to keep a sense of humor and to go easy on yourself. You are doing the best you can—and you are learning and growing all along the way, even if it doesn't always feel that way.

RECOVERY IS A PROCESS.

My esteemed colleague Joyce Marter, owner of Urban Balance, LLC describes life progress as being filled with backloops, not a consistent movement forward. This is so true.

Positive change is not linear. You may feel as if you are going backward at times—and you might be right, but that's part of how real life progress happens. Fake change happens overnight. Real, long-lasting changes take time, and they include lots of setbacks. As you embark upon this journey, you can expect to take a step or two backward for every few steps you take forward.

The good news is, you will always be given opportunities to give it away. So you will get plenty of practice. The bad news is the same as the good: you will always be given opportunities to give it away. It won't consistently be easy to walk away from those detrimental caretaking opportunities. The difference is, now you can see them coming, and you have the tools to deal with them. So embrace the challenge, and when you do make those little steps and big leaps forward, celebrate them!

Afterword

"Embrace yesterday's foundation, today's successes,
tomorrow's possibilities."
—Twelve-step literature

By now, you have realized where you have been giving it away and you know what to do about it. However, before you get too aggressively into go-do-and-change mode, Got It Girl, take it easy. Congratulate yourself for finishing the book and for learning important new tools and insights.

Awareness is power. You have that now. This will take you anywhere you need to go. You are ready to forge your new path and enjoy the beauty of what your new life has to offer.

Don't go spending any time beating up on yourself or feeling bad about some of the places you have been and the decisions you have made before. They have all served the purpose of getting you to where you are now, the place where you need to be. Make amends to yourself today if you are carrying any of that unearned guilt and shame, whereby you acknowledge and forgive yourself for how you have treated yourself. Then, onward!

CHERILYNN'S DAILY LIVING TIPS

---

1. Start each day with a devotion, a quiet moment of reflection and/or prayer, and set your intention for the day.

2. Seek help and support for putting into action each step of your plan to get it back.

3. Have compassion for yourself, and give yourself time to make these changes. Many, many backloops, remember?

4. Stay in the moment. Mindfulness is a powerful here-and-now tool.

5. Keep focused on what you want and what is possible.

6. Push away and close the door on negative, hopeless, and powerless thinking.

7. Take time each day for quiet, meditation, prayer, or solitude.

8. When you are superstressed and do not have time to do the above, try some belly breathing and clear your mind for just a few minutes. It makes a huge difference stress-wise on your body.

9. End each day with a gratefulness list. Make sure you put yourself in there. Give yourself some back-pats before you go to sleep.

10. Rely on others if the day is particularly hard.

11. Call someone and laugh at the ridiculousness of it all (and at yourself, even).

12. Surround yourself with people whom you love and care about, and who support you.

Lastly, thank you so much for buying this book and reading this information. I am honored that you chose *Stop Giving It Away* to take up some of your precious time. It means so much to me. If you want added support, reach out, join my Facebook group, join the blog, and give me your feedback. I know there is a lot I can learn from you as well.

And, as always . . .

Take care,
Cherilynn

ACKNOWLEDGMENTS

This book is the result of a tremendous amount of effort from so many people.

First, I want to thank the She Writes Press staff in California for their awesome job helping me to publish this baby: Brooke Warner, who is the publisher of She Writes Press, as well as Krissa, Cait, Tali, and Barrett. I can't say enough good things about the publishing process with this committed team.

I also want to thank Crystal with BookSparks; Sara Connell, who helped me move to the next step; Melody Beattie, an incredible writer who has inspired millions, including me; and Lou Carlozo, a talented journalist, editor, and writing coach, whose faith from the beginning helped me bring this book to fruition.

Thanks also to the following people:

My wonderful family.

Todd and John.

My incredible friends—I am so lucky to have such a nurturing (and fun) support system.

My mom and dad—your love has always been deeply felt.

My awesome hubby, who cheered me on.

My wonderful boys, Collin and Wesley, who give me the greatest joy.

My dog, Christy—I miss you.

Stephanie D.

Joyce Marter, a colleague and bestie, whose advocacy and encouragement powered me forward. (Joyce, I couldn't do this whole "life thing" without you!)

My clients, past, present, and future, whom I adore and learn so much from.

And last but not least, thank you, Liz Carey, my author product development specialist. Without her creative/editing/coaching partnership, this book would never have rocked like it does!

And foremost, I give gratitude to my Higher Power, through whom all things are possible.

RESOURCES AND
RECOMMENDED READING

I reference several resources throughout *Stop Giving It Away*. These and other titles listed here may also help you in your journey.

Bass, Ellen, and Laura Davis. *The Courage to Heal: A Guide for Women Survivors of Child Sexual Abuse: 20th Anniversary Edition.* New York: HarperCollins, 2008.

Beattie, Melody. *Codependent No More: How to Stop Controlling Others and Start Caring for Yourself.* Center City, MN: Hazelden, 1992.

Beattie, Melody. *The New Codependency: Help and Guidance for Today's Generation.* New York: Simon & Schuster, 2009.

Behary, Wendy T. *Disarming the Narcissist. Surviving and Thriving with the Self-Absorbed.* Oakland, CA: New Harbinger Publications, 2013.

Bradshaw, John. *Healing the Shame That Binds You.* Deerfield Beach, FL: Health Communications, 1989.

Brown, Brené. *The Gifts of Imperfection: Let Go of Who You Think You're Supposed to Be and Embrace Who You Are.* Center City, MN: Hazelden, 2010.

Cameron, Julia. *The Artist's Way: A Spiritual Path to Higher Creativity.* Los Angeles, CA: Jeremy P. Tarcher/Perigee, 1992.

Carnes, Patrick, and Joseph Moriarity. *Sexual Anorexia: Overcoming Sexual Self-Hatred.* Center City, MN: Hazelden, 1997.

Carson, Richard David. *Taming Your Gremlin: A Surprisingly Simple Method for Getting out of Your Own Way.* New York: Quill, 2003.

Carnes, Patrick, and Joseph Moriarity. *Sexual Anorexia: Overcoming Sexual Self-Hatred.* Center City, MN: Hazelden, 1997.

Carter, Jimmy. *A Call to Action: Women, Religion, Violence, and Power.* New York: Simon & Schuster, 2014.

Cloud, Dr. Henry, and Dr. John Townsend. *Boundaries: When to Say Yes, How to Say No.* Waterville, MA: Walker, 2004.

Dyer, Wayne W. *Wishes Fulfilled: Mastering the Art of Manifesting.* Carlsbad, CA: Hay House, 2012.

Englander, Arlene. *The In-Sourcing Handbook: Where and How to Find the Happiness You Deserve.* North Charleston, SC: CreateSpace, 2012.

Evans, Patricia. *The Verbally Abusive Relationship: How to Recognize It and How to Respond.* Holbrook, MA: Adams Media Corporation, 1996.

Golden, Stephanie. *Slaying the Mermaid: Women and the Culture of Sacrifice.* New York: Harmony, 1998.

Kay, Katty. *The Confidence Code: The Art and Science of Self-Assurance—and What Women Need to Know.* New York: Harper Business, 2014.

Hunter, Erika M. *Little Book of Big Emotions: How Five Feelings Affect Everything You Do (and Don't Do).* Center City, MN: Hazelden, 2004.

Huffington, Arianna. *Thrive: The Third Metric to Redefining Success and Creating a Life of Well-Being, Wisdom, and Wonder.* New York: Harmony Books, 2014.

Khalsa, Dharma Singh, and Cameron Stauth. *Meditation as Medicine: Activate the Power of Your Natural Healing Force.* New York: Pocket, 2001.

Lancer, Darlene. *Conquering Shame and Codependency: 8 Steps to Freeing the True You.* Center City, MN: Hazelden, 2011.

Lerner, Harriet Goldhor. *The Dance of Anger.* New York: Harper & Row, 1989.

Levine, Peter A. *Waking the Tiger: Healing Trauma—the Innate Capacity to Transform Overwhelming Experiences.* Berkeley, CA: North Atlantic, 1997.

Levine, Peter A., and Maggie Kline. *Trauma Through a Child's Eyes: Awakening the Ordinary Miracle of Healing.* Berkeley, CA: North Atlantic, 2006.

Magli, Ida. *Women and Self-Sacrifice in the Christian Church: A Cultural History from the First to the Nineteenth Century.* Jefferson, NC: McFarland, 2003.

Miller, Alice, and Ruth Neils Ward. *The Drama of the Gifted Child: The Search for the True Self.* New York: Basic Books, 1997.

Rosenberg, Ross. *The Human Magnet Syndrome: Why We Love People Who Hurt Us.* Eau Claire, WI: PESI Publishing & Media, 2013.

Sandberg, Sheryl. *Lean In: Women, Work, and the Will to Lead.* New York: Random House, 2013.

Stoop, David, and Stephen Arterburn. *The Life Recovery Bible.* Carol Stream, IL: Tyndale House, 1998.

Tolle, Eckhart. *A New Earth: Awakening to Your Life's Purpose.* New York: Plume, 2006.

Ullman, Sarah E. *Talking About Sexual Assault: Society's Response to Survivors.* Washington, DC: American Psychological Association, 2010.

Anything else by Hazelden or Al-Anon's conference-approved twelve-step literature

SOURCES AND RESEARCH

Copious research supports implicit bias and gender shaping, women and self-sacrifice as a gender expectation, and other topics covered in *Stop Giving It Away*. However, this book is intended for the general reading public.

—C. Veland, LCSW, MSW

CHAPTER 1
WHAT IS A GIVEAWAY GIRL?
WHAT IS GIVING IT AWAY?

1. Wendy T. Behary, *Disarming the Narcissist. Surviving and Thriving with the Self-Absorbed* (Oakland, CA: New Harbinger Publications, 2013).

2. Catalyst, Inc., "The Double-Bind Dilemma for Women in Leadership: Damned If You Do, Doomed If You Don't," report (New York: Catalyst, 2007).

3. Kathleen C. Basile et al., "National Intimate Partner and Sexual Violence Survey 2010 Summary Report" (Atlanta, GA: Centers for Disease Control and Prevention, National Center for Injury Prevention and Control, Division of Violence Prevention, 2011).

4. Mental Health Foundation, "Mental Health Statistics: Men & Women," accessed September 28, 2014, http://www. mentalhealth.org.uk/help-information/mental-health-statistics/ men-women/.

5. World Health Organization, "Gender and Women's Mental Health," accessed September 26, 2014, http://www.who.int/ mental_health/prevention/genderwomen/en/.

CHAPTER 2
DETRIMENTAL CARETAKING

1. US Department of Labor, Bureau of Labor Statistics, "Household Data, Annual Averages, Table 39," report, accessed March 2014, http://bls.gov/cps/cpsaat39.htm.

2. Family Caregiver Alliance, "Women and Caregiving: Facts and Figures," accessed September 28, 2014, https://www.caregiver.org/women-and-caregiving-facts-and-figures.

3. P. S. Arno, "The Economic Value of Informal Caregiving, U.S., 2000," paper presented at the annual meeting of the American Association for Geriatric Psychiatry, Florida, February 2002.

4. Suzanne M. Bianchi, John P. Robinson, and Melissa A. Milkie, *Changing Rhythms of American Family Life* (New York: Russell Sage Foundation, 2006).

5. Centers for Disease Control and Prevention, National Center for Injury Prevention and Control, Division of Violence Prevention, "Prevalence and Characteristics of Sexual Violence, Stalking, and Intimate Partner Violence and Victimization—National Intimate Partner and Sexual Violence Survey," report, 2011.

6. Melody Beattie, *Codependent No More: How to Stop Controlling Others and Start Caring for Yourself* (Center City, MN: Hazelden, 1992).

CHAPTER 3
GIVE AWAY MOMS

1. Elizabeth Mendes, Lydia Saad, and Kyle McGeeney, "Stay-at-Home Moms Report More Depression, Sadness, Anger, but

Low-Income Stay-at-Home Moms Struggle the Most," report (Washington, DC: Gallup, 2012).

2. Molly Ladd-Taylor and Lauri Umansky, *Bad Mothers: The Politics of Blame in Twentieth-Century America* (New York: New York University Press, 1988).

3. PBS, "Refrigerator Mothers: History of Autism Blame," in *POV: Documentaries with a Point of View*, July 16, 2002.

4. UN News Center, "Fourth World Conference on Women, Beijing 1995," accessed September 27, 2014, http://www.un.org/womenwatch/daw/beijing/platform/poverty.htm.

5. Olivia Morgan and Karen Skelton, "The Shriver Report Executive Summary," January 2014, accessed September 28, 2014, http://www.americanprogress.org/issues/economy/report/2014/01/12/81906/the-shriver-report-a-womans-nation-pushes-back-from-the-brink/.

6. M. A. Milkie, S. B. Raley, and S. M. Bianchi, "Taking on the Second Shift: Time Allocations and Time Pressures of U.S. Parents with Preschoolers," *Social Forces* 88, no. 2 (2009): 487–517, DOI: 10.1353/sof.0.0268.

7. Gale Berkowitz, "Study on Friendship Among Women: An Alternative to Fight or Flight," report (Los Angeles: UCLA, 2002).

CHAPTER 4

GIVEAWAY WIVES AND GIRLFRIENDS

1. Karyn Loscocco and Susan Walzer, "Gender and the Culture of Heterosexual Marriage in the United States," *Journal of Family Theory & Review* 5, no. 1 (2013): 1–14, DOI: 10.1111/jftr.12003.

2. Vicky Larsen, "Why Women and Men Don't Have the Same Marriage," *Huffington Post*. April 2014, accessed September 29, 2014, http://www.huffingtonpost.com/vicki-larson/his-hers-marriage_b_3129269.html.

3. Open Society Foundations, "Defining the Addiction Treatment Gap: Data Summary," November 2010.

CHAPTER 5

GIVEAWAY GIRLS IN CAREER

1. Andy Barr, "2010 Complete Election Coverage: Hillary Clinton: I'd Have Hired Barack Obama," accessed September 27, 2014, http://www.politico.com/news/stories/1009/28278. html.

2. Oprah.com, "Oprah Talks to Condoleezza Rice," accessed September 28, 2014, http://www.oprah.com/omagazine/Oprah-Interviews-Condoleezza-Rice.

3. Morgan and Skelton, "The Shriver Report Executive Summary."

4. F. Crosby, "The Denial of Personal Discrimination," *American Behavioral Scientist* 27, no. 3 (1984): 371–86, DOI: 10.1177/000276484027003008.

5. Daniel Goleman, *Emotional Intelligence* (New York: Bantam Books, 1995).

6. Katty Kay, *The Confidence Code: The Art and Science of Self-Assurance—and What Women Need to Know* (New York: Harper Business, 2014).

7. Katty Kay and Claire Shipman, "The Confidence Gap," *The Atlantic*, April 14, 2014.

8. Garcia-Retamero, R., & López-Zafra, E. (2006). Prejudice against women in male-congenial environments: Perceptions of gender role congruity in leadership. *Sex Roles, 55,* 51-61.

9. Moss-Racusin, C. A., Dovidio, J. F., Brescoll, V. L., Graham, M., & Handelsman, J. (2012). Science faculty's subtle gender biases favor male students. *Proceedings of the National Academy of Sciences, 109,* 16474-16479.

10. Maria Konnikova, "Lean Out: The Dangers for Women Who Negotiate." *The New Yorker,* June 10, 2014, accessed September 29, 2014, http://www.newyorker.com/science/maria-konnikova/lean-out-the-dangers-for-women-who-negotiate.

CHAPTER 6

WHAT SHAPES A GIRL'S ROLE IN THE WORLD

1. US Department of Labor, Bureau of Labor Statistics, "Household Data, Annual Averages, Table 39."

2. Family Caregiver Alliance, "Women and Caregiving: Facts and Figures," accessed September 28, 2014, https://www.caregiver.org/women-and-caregiving-facts-and-figures.

3. Arno, "The Economic Value of Informal Caregiving."

4. Omolade Alawode, "How Your Zip Code Can Affect Your Weight," IQ Solutions, accessed April 8, 2014, http://www.iqsolutions.com/ideas-and-insights/blog/how-your-zip-code-can-affect-your-weight.

5. Peter A. Levine, *Waking the Tiger: Healing Trauma: The Innate Capacity to Transform Overwhelming Experiences* (Berkeley, CA: North Atlantic, 1997).

6. Beattie, *Codependent No More.*

7. Alice Miller and Ruth Neils Ward, *The Drama of the Gifted Child: The Search for the True Self* (New York: Basic Books, 1997).

8. Elinor J. Brecher, "Crossing 'Confidence Gap' Poses High Hurdle for Girls," *Knight Ridder/Tribune News Service*, October 5, 1994, accessed September 28, 2014, http://www.highbeam.com/doc/1G1-15787055.html?refid=easy_hf.

9. (Second study) The Dove Self-Esteem Fund, "Real Girls, Real Pressure: A National Report on the State of Self-Esteem," June 2008, accessed September 30, 2014, http://www.isacs.org/misc_files/SelfEsteem_Report%20-%20Dove%20Campaign%20for%20Real%20Beauty.pdf.

10. Ruth Perou et al., "Depression More Prevalent in Girls Than Boys"; Centers for Disease Control and Prevention, "Mental Health Surveillance Among Children—United States, 2005–2011," May 17, 2013, accessed September 30, 2014, http://www.cdc.gov/mmwr/preview/mmwrhtml/su6202a1.htm?s_cid=su6202a1_w#Tab7.

11. Ariane Hegewisch and Hannah Liepmann, "The Gender Wage Gap: 2010" (Washington, D.C.: Institute for Women's Policy Research, March 2010), http://webcache.googleusercontent.com/search?q=cache:RFkx-23jV8IJ:www.iwpr.org/publications/pubs/the-gender-wage-gap-2010/at_download/file+&cd=1&hl=en&ct=clnk&gl=us&client= firefox-a.

12. The White House Project, "The White House Project Report: Benchmarking Women's Leadership," report, June 24, 2009, http://www.in.gov/icw/files/benchmark_wom_leadership.pdf.

13. Organization for Economic Cooperation and Development, "Occupations of men and women," 2004. http://webcache.googleusercontent.com/search?q=cache39ezWm

1O1T0J:www.oecd.org/std/37964549.pdf+&cd=2&hl=en&ct=
clnk&gl=us&client=firefox-a.

14. Joan Williams and Nancy Segal, "The New Glass Ceiling:
Mothers—and Fathers—Sue for Discrimination" (Washington,
D.C.: American University, November 2002).

15. Steven D. Levitt and Stephen J. Dubner, *Freakonomics: A
Rogue Economist Explores the Hidden Side of Everything* (New
York: William Morrow, 2005).

16. Kathleen C. Basile et al., "National Intimate Partner and
Sexual Violence Survey 2010 Summary Report."

17. Bobbie Mixon, "Chore Wars: Men, Women and Housework," National Science Foundation, April 28, 2008. http://
www.nsf.gov/discoveries/disc_summ.jsp?org=NSF&cntn_id=
111458&preview=false.

18. Ida Magli, *Women and Self-sacrifice in the Christian Church:
A Cultural History from the First to the Nineteenth Century*
(Jefferson, NC: McFarland, 2003).

19. Stephanie Golden, *Slaying the Mermaid: Women and the
Culture of Sacrifice* (New York: Harmony, 1998).

20. Sean Smith, "Goddess of War," *Entertainment Weekly*,
January 1, 2010, http://www.ew.com/ew/article/0,,2033
3854,00.html.

CHAPTER 7

FROM GIVEAWAY GIRLS TO GOT IT GIRLS

1. Nick Tasler, "What Is Your Momentum Factor?" *Psychology
Today*, August 30, 2012, http://www.psychologytoday.com/
blog/strategic-thinking/201208/what-is-your-momentum-
factor.

2. Brian Wansink and Jeffrey Sobal, "Mindless Eating: The 200 Daily Food Decisions We Overlook," *Environment and Behavior* 39, no. 1 (2007): 106–23.

CHAPTER 8
GOT IT GIRLS: BOUNDARIES

1. Anne Pickwick, "Most US Men Believe PMS Is a Normal Part of a Woman's Cycle," *Medical News Today*, January 26, 2005, http://www.medicalnewstoday.com/releases/19302.php.

2. Al-Alon Family Group Headquarters, Inc., "Detachment," brochure from Al-Anon's Conference Approved Literature.

CHAPTER 9
YOU: SELF-CARE FOR YOUR MIND, BODY, AND SPIRIT

1. Centers for Disease Control and Prevention, "Leading Causes of Death in Females United States, 2010 (current listing)," accessed on October 31, 2013, http://www.cdc.gov/women/lcod/2010/index.htm.

2. American Heart Association, "Causes and Prevention of Heart Disease," 2014, https://www.goredforwomen.org/about-heart-disease/facts_about_heart_disease_in_women-sub-category/causes-prevention/.

3. American Institute of Stress, "Stress Effects," 2014, http://www.stress.org/stress-effects/.

4. Kirsi Ahola et al., "Work-Related Exhaustion and Telomere Length: A Population-Based Study." *PLOS ONE* 7, no. 7 (2012), http://www.plosone.org/article/info%3Adoi%2F10.1371%2Fjournal.pone.0040186.

5. David McNamee, "Gender-Specific Research Has 'Improved Heart Disease Diagnosis in Women," *Medical News Today,* June 17, 2014, http://www.medicalnewstoday.com/articles/278325.php.

6. Carolyn Thomas, "Heart Attack Misdiagnosis in Women," *Heart Sisters* (blog), May 28, 2009, http://myheartsisters.org/2009/05/28/heart-attack-misdiagnosis-women/.

7. J. Hector Pope, et al., "Missed Diagnoses of Acute Cardiac Ischemia in the Emergency Department," *New England Journal of Medicine* 342 (April 20, 2000): 1163–1170, http://www.nejm.org/doi/full/10.1056/NEJM200004203421603.

8. Diane E. Hoffman and Anita J. Tarzian, "The Girl Who Cried Pain: A Bias Against Women in the Treatment of Pain," *Journal of Law, Medicine and Ethics* 29, no. 1 (spring 2001): 13–27.

9. Patrick Carnes and Joseph Moriarity, *Sexual Anorexia: Overcoming Sexual Self-Hatred* (Center City, MN: Hazelden, 1997).

10. Dharma Singh Khalsa and Cameron Stauth, *Meditation as Medicine: Activate the Power of Your Natural Healing Force* (New York: Pocket, 2001).

11. Englander, *The In-Sourcing Handbook.*

CHAPTER 10

LETTING GO WHEN IT'S HARD TO LET GO

1. Spencer Johnson, *Who Moved My Cheese?: An Amazing Way to Deal with Change in Your Work and in Your Life* (New York: Putnam, 1998).

2. Sue Langly and Sophie Francis, "The Neuroscience of Change: Why It's Difficult and What Makes It Easier," Langley Group, accessed May 23, 2012, http://www.langley group.

com.au/articles/the-neuroscience-of-change—why-it-s-difficult
-and-what-makes-it-easier.html.

3. P. Lally et al., "How are habits formed: Modeling habit
formation in the real world," *European Journal of Social Psychology* 40, no. 6 (2010): 998–1009, DOI: 10.1002/ejsp.674.

4. Rick Nauert, "Modeling Behavior for Children Has Long-
Lasting Effects," *Psych Central*, May 28, 2010, accessed
September 30, 2014, http://psychcentral.com/news/2010/05/27/
modeling-behavior-for-children-has-long-lasting-effects/14139.
html.

5. Martha Nibley Beck, *Finding Your Way in a Wild New
World: Four Steps to Fulfilling Your True Calling* (London:
Piatkus, 2012).

ABOUT THE AUTHOR

CHERILYNN M. VELAND, LCSW, MSW, leads a new self-advocacy movement intended to help women reach out, speak up, and take action steps for what's best for them. She is the author of *Stop Giving It Away* and a Chicago-based psychotherapist and social worker who has been helping individuals, couples and families for more than 20 years.

Cherilynn has dealt with a wide variety of mental health issues and challenges as a result of her work with battered women and sexual assault victims, psychiatric hospitals and outpatient settings. She has worked in corporate settings and nonprofit institutions and is founder and owner of Lincoln Park Counseling in Chicago, Illinois.

Cherilynn offers self-advocacy workshops and training seminars, as well as in-person and online coaching and counseling services for individuals and groups.

For more information or to arrange a speaking engagement or workshop, contact Cherilynn at cherilynnveland@gmail.com

Printed in the United States
by Baker & Taylor Publisher Services